AF291930

Memoir of a Polish Resistance Fighter

Memoir of a Polish Resistance Fighter

Defying Nazi and Russian Occupation in World War II

Stanislaw Franciszek Czekaj
with Len Czekaj

Pen & Sword
MILITARY

First published in Great Britain in 2026 by
Pen & Sword Military
An imprint of Pen & Sword Books Limited
Yorkshire – Philadelphia

ISBN 978 1 03619 382 9

A CIP catalogue record for this book is
available from the British Library.

Typeset by Mac Style
Printed in the UK by CPI Group (UK) Ltd, Croydon, CR0 4YY.

The Publisher's authorised representative in the EU for product
safety is Authorised Rep Compliance Ltd., Ground Floor,
71 Lower Baggot Street, Dublin D02 P593, Ireland.
www.arccompliance.com

For a complete list of Pen & Sword titles please contact:

PEN & SWORD BOOKS LIMITED
47 Church Street, Barnsley, South Yorkshire, S70 2AS, England
E-mail: enquiries@pen-and-sword.co.uk
Website: www.pen-and-sword.co.uk
or
PEN AND SWORD BOOKS
1950 Lawrence Road, Havertown, PA 19083, USA
E-mail: uspen-and-sword@casematepublishers.com
Website: www.penandswordbooks.com

Contents

THE CZEKAJ FAMILY TREE

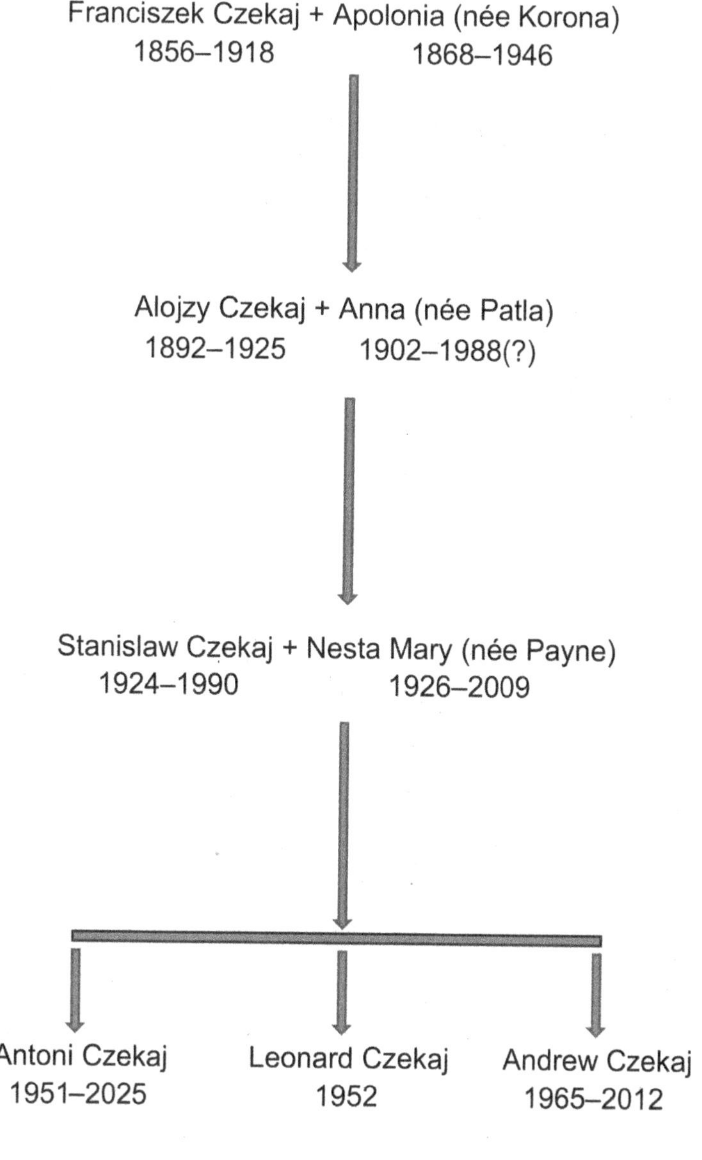

Historical Note

On the eve of the Second World War, Poland found itself in a precarious position, caught in the middle of two opposing and increasingly dominant superpowers – Nazi Germany in the West and Soviet Russia in the East – each fuelled by a potent ideology, staking its claim to supremacy over Europe.

Against this backdrop of invasion and occupation in September 1939, first by Germany and then Russia, the Polish Government-in-Exile was formed in Paris (later relocating to London), while the Polish Underground State was established on the ground. These institutions denounced Poland's foreign occupiers, regarding their imposition through force to be illegal under international law.

By extension, the formation of an armed Resistance represented a legitimate right to resist against foreign aggression. Partisan units were assembled with a directive of sabotage against the enemy. The Union of Armed Struggle (*Związek Walki Zbrojnej*) was established in 1939. This Resistance movement later formed the basis of the Polish Home Army (*Armia Krajowa*) in February 1942.

It was a highly organized movement, with a hierarchical command structure, reporting to the Government-in-Exile. Nevertheless, in practice, by nature of operating covertly while under occupation, life-or-death decisions often had to be made in haste by the operatives on the ground.

Merciless atrocities committed by both German and Russian occupiers were common knowledge during Poland's occupation, from Gestapo shootings and rumoured Nazi death camps, to mass execution of Polish intelligentsia and prisoners of war by Soviet forces at Katyn Forest.

To modern sensibility, many of the actions described in this book – on all sides – appear brutal in the extreme. They are a reflection of the violent times, in which a Polish Resistance fighter's capture by Nazi or Soviet agents would result in near-certain death. One atrocity doesn't justify another, though extreme measures were borne out by the existential threat both on an individual and national level.

When the fighting ceased in 1945, the post-war peace treaties saw Poland formally brought under Soviet control. The 'Trial of the Sixteen' – a show trial orchestrated by the Soviet Union in Moscow and designed to discredit the Resistance – saw key political members of the Polish Underground State put on trial on trumped-up charges including state terrorism and Nazi collaboration, with the majority convicted. Some had short prison sentences followed by exile; others died in prison – possibly murdered. This event put the fate of the Resistance cause into sharp relief.

Long after the war had ended, ongoing Soviet influence ensured that the role of the Resistance remained highly controversial within Poland. In the decades that followed, Resistance and Home Army members were denounced and persecuted by the communist regime as traitors and criminals. Millions of Poles went under investigation by the NKDV (the Russian secret police) and its successor organizations. Up to 6,000 Poles connected to the armed struggle were executed through the courts, with many more dying in prison. Others were either forced into hiding or exile, in fear of their lives.

Meanwhile, the Polish Government-in-Exile continued to recognize and honour the Resistance from its headquarters in London. Only since the liberation and independence of Poland, at the end of 1989, has the Resistance been officially legitimized within the country itself, and hence examined more widely.

Timeline

11 November 1918	The First World War ends and Poland gains independence, following over 120 years of subjugation by foreign powers; the date is commemorated as National Independence Day
23 August 1939	The Molotov-Ribbentrop Pact is signed by the Soviet Union and Germany, a non-aggression agreement that facilitates the partition of Poland
1 September 1939	Germany invades Poland from the West; Britain declares war on Germany within 48 hours
September 1939	The Polish Government-in-Exile is established in Paris, later relocating to London following the fall of France in June 1940
16 September 1939	Poland's military commander, Marshal Rydz-Smigly issues the order for Poland to organize Partisan groups
17 September 1939	The Soviet Union invades Poland from the East
18 September 1939	Marshal Rydz-Smigly flees to Romania; Polish Resistance groups begin to assemble in the country's capital, Warsaw
6 October 1939	The last Polish Army forces are defeated by the German Army at the Battle of Kock, paving the way for partition
April–May 1940	Thousands of Polish PoWs are executed in the Katyn Forest, Russia
22 June 1941	Germany invades the Soviet Union in Operation Barbarossa, ending their non-aggression pact

14 February 1942	The Polish Home Army (*Armia Krajowa*) is formed, out of the Polish Resistance, in allegiance with the exiled government
13 April 1943	Germany announces the discovery of the Katyn Forest massacre and identifies Soviet responsibility
January 1944–January 1945	The Home Army organizes a series of uprisings against German occupiers, known as Operation Tempest
1 August 1944	The Warsaw Uprising begins against German occupation, lasting until the beginning of October; its failure leads to the decimation of the city, and the deportation and execution of thousands of Poles at Nazi death camps
8 May 1945	The war in Europe ends, with Poland remaining under the auspices of the Soviet Union
18 June 1945	The Trial of the Sixteen is staged against key political figures of the Polish Underground State for crimes against the Soviet Union; over the ensuing 45 years, the Polish Government-in-Exile and the Polish Resistance are officially denounced by the ruling communist government in Poland; thousands of Resistance fighters are sentenced to death
9 November 1989	The Berlin Wall is torn down, symbolizing the fall of communism in Eastern Europe
December 1989	Poland regains its independence with the establishment of the democratic Third Polish Republic; the decriminalizing of the historic role of the Resistance begins
16 October 1992	The new Polish government officially recognizes the honours bestowed upon Resistance members during occupation

My Tribute – A Preface

by Len Czekaj

Firstly, I would like to give my sincere thanks to my wife's cousin, military historian Peter Cottrell, for encouraging me to dig out my father Stanislaw's manuscript of his life story and retype it, and for all the research he has undertaken in searching for the war records of my grandfather's capture and subsequent incarceration in a Russian prisoner-of-war camp during the First World War. The entire text about my grandfather (Stan's father), Alojzy Czekaj, is wholly Peter Cottrell's work.

Peter was commissioned into the Royal Navy as a lieutenant in 1988 and transferred to the Regular Army in 1995. He served in Bosnia, Northern Ireland, Iraq and Afghanistan. After leaving the army in 2008 as a major, he then taught English, History, Latin and Classics in St John's School, Marlborough, before becoming head of English and Media at Kirkby Stephen Grammar School in Cumbria. He is now retired.

He has had three books on Irish history published – *The Anglo-Irish War*, *The Irish Civil War* and *The War for Ireland*, as well as three novels – *England's Janissary*, *The Lambs* and *Wyrdgrove*.

In his book, my father Stanislaw Franciszek Czekaj, who was from the village of Glowienka, tells of the events that he lived through before, during, and after Poland was occupied, first by the Germans and then the Russians. He tells of his time in the Polish Resistance and how he managed to evade capture, even though he had a price on his head and was wanted dead or alive.

To stay safe, he made his way to the West and had various escapades on his way through Germany and Belgium, finally making his way to Britain and finding work in the West Country. He ended up in Cardiff and married my mother, Nesta. He wrote about his whole life, only stopping a few weeks before he died on 12 August 1990, two days after his sixty-sixth birthday.

His dying wish was that someday his story would be published. These manuscripts (all six of them), as well as thirteen audio tapes on which he dictated his book, are now with the Podkarpakie Museum in Krosno, Poland, along with his medals, war documents and photographs, as I felt that they could be properly preserved as a valuable resource for research.

Also, my sincere thanks to Czeslaw Nowak, the Vice President of the Podkarpackie Historical Society, who incorporated Stan's original manuscript with a lot of other material added relating to Stan and his family in a Polish book, titled *Pomiedzy Zlem A Zlem* (*Between Evil and Evil*).

The path to the publication of Stan's story was by pure chance. A young Polish journalist student from Cardiff University saw my nephew Chris Czekaj playing rugby for Wales and the commentator mentioned that he had a Polish grandfather.

She decided to look further into this and interviewed my mother Nesta. A story was printed in the local newspaper, the *South Wales Echo*, and *The Polish Times* later picked it up. Subsequently, I was contacted by Czeslaw Nowak asking me if I had any information on Stan. I provided digital copies of all the material I had, and the book *Pomiedzy Zlem A Zlem* was published sometime later.

The following memoir recounts Stan's incredible story, as told from his own perspective. As such, the opinions and claims expressed throughout his recollections reflect his personal experiences and insights.

Prologue

For years I had the intention to write my memoirs of my eventful life, especially the war years under German, then Russian occupation. Eventually, after forty years, I have decided to do it. Although everything will be written as it was, the sequence of events and dates may in some cases not be exact. There are many things that I have forgotten, but I will try to portray life and conditions in pre-war Poland during both occupations, escaping to the West, life in DP (or displaced person camps), joining the Polish Provisional Brigade (*Brygasa Swietokrzyska*), then emigration to the Belgian coal mines and eventually to Great Britain.

Most of what is written can still be verified as many people I have mentioned in this book are still alive. [Many of the people Stan mentioned have since passed away.] I also have letters, documents and photographs to confirm the authenticity of the names and places that are mentioned.

I hope it will illustrate the terrible hunger, hardship and fear we had to endure in these long years. As my English is self-taught, there may be some grammatical errors for which I hope readers will forgive me.

Stanislaw Franciszek Czekaj (1924–1990)

1

In the Beginning

What is in the first part cannot be verified but it has stuck in my memory so I must write it. It could be dream, imagination or fact. A stream of light and energy, more like a flame, flowing continuously from east to west on the right side of the Himalayas and approximately 30 degrees higher; weakening as it reached the west, but appearing to circle the Earth.

My being was in that stream.

My destination was Jaslo town but – as if on order – I stopped in what seemed to be grey clouds or mist. I do not know how long I was there, but then I descended to what must have been my mother's womb. It was quiet and comfortable. But then I became restless. It must have been time to be born. It was a painful, suffocating feeling; then relief. I was born on 10 August 1924.

Sometimes, I sensed my mother crying, then the milk from her breast was bitter. I once felt my father leaning over me saying, '*Stasiu*', the familiar form of my name, Stanislaw, but I could not answer because I could not speak yet. I can't remember my father (Alojzy Czekaj). He died on 25 February 1925.

2

My Parents and Their Families

My mother Anna's maiden name was Patla. Her parents were Maria and Franciszek. She had two brothers, Ludwik and Antoni, also a sister, Jozia. They were a poor family.

Grandfather and the elder brother, Ludwik, emigrated to America to earn some money. After a few years Grandfather came back. But Ludwik stayed and joined the army. He was sent to the Philippines and that's the last we heard of him.

My father's family was much larger. There were thirteen children – seven sons and six daughters. My father was the youngest of the sons and the last of the sons to die. He contracted tuberculosis in a Russian prisoner-of-war camp during the First World War. I remember three of his sisters: Franka, the eldest, whose married name was Kolanko and had seven daughters; Stefka, an unmarried teacher; and Hania, who married a nice man named Wilk and together they had two children, Wieslaw and Halina.

My father's family were sufficiently wealthy. They owned a large water mill (of which I can remember the ruins and the wheel), many hectares of forest and land, some of which I inherited. I remember my mother used to take me around and show me which of it was mine. She used to rent it out as she could not cultivate it all.

My grandmother (my father's mother) was a very hard woman. She never shed a tear for any of her ten dead children. She was also nasty to my mother as she did not approve of my father's marriage to a poor family. My mother could stand this no longer, so she went to live with her parents.

The grandmother sacked a faithful servant who had been in service for many years with the family. He vowed revenge and one Easter Sunday, when all the family were in church, there was a fire which destroyed all the premises, the mill, the stables, thirty cows, twenty-four pigs, six horses and dozens of chickens, ducks, geese and turkeys. Everybody suspected the servant, but I don't know whether he was convicted of it.

3

Temporary Life with Mother's Parents

My mother moved with me to her parents' home which was on the other side of the village called Tloki, about two miles away. However, things did not work out as planned. Her sister, Jozia, got married, and all of us were living in that very small house. Her husband wasn't a very nice man and did not get on with my grandfather, so something had to be done. My mother borrowed dollars from people who had relatives in America and was determined to have her own house. She sacrificed her life for me.

She was a very beautiful woman and was elected beauty queen before she was married. She was a beautiful widow at 21 years of age and refused many offers of marriage and emigration to America. That was a great sacrifice. She borrowed enough money to buy the material for the house. It was to be a wooden house like most of them in the village.

I was 18 months old when my grandmother Patla died, but I remember clearly that she used to hang her walking stick on the door. I remember when the carpenters started squaring the logs. First, they soaked a long piece of string in a bucket containing charcoal mixed with water then stretched it and flicked it, thus obtaining a straight line. Using a *Topors* axe with a short handle and about a 12–15″ blade, they made the logs square then put them in a stack to dry.

Eventually they built our home. When the roof trusses were in place, they put a *Wiecha* or 'topping out' (a bunch of decorated branches) on the end of the roof, a sign that the main structure was completed. The house was the shape of a bungalow. There were seven rooms: a kitchen/dining room and grandfather's bed in one room; the next room was my mother's and my bedroom; next was a small bedroom and a hallway; behind them was a stall and storeroom.

Right at the end, stretching the entire width of the house, was a large room for threshing corn. Behind the house was a wooden toilet, then there was a dug out, a square hole, approximately 5m by 5m by 0.5m deep, for storing manure.

The house was approximately 12m long by 8m wide, with one front and one back door. The roof was made of red tiles. There were gaps between the logs, which were filled with clay mixed with moss and oat flakes pressed into the gaps then painted with lime. It did not shrink. Grandfather's bed was a wooden sofa which pulled out to make a bed, otherwise it was like a bench. We had no floorboards yet, only flattened-out earth. There was a table and a couple of wooden benches by the table. I used to kneel by the bench saying my prayers. In the hall there were stairs to the loft, where we used to keep hay and corn before threshing, and then the straw that was left from the threshing.

In the kitchen there was a range where my mother used to cook our meals. Behind it was an oven for baking bread. Almost every house had one. The dough was mixed in a *Koryto*, a boat-like vessel carved out of poplar wood, approximately 5ft long by 2ft wide and 18in deep, with two handles on each end.

The dough was made out of corn flour, enough for twelve large round loaves. The bread had to be eaten until it was all gone. There was no waste.

For lighting, we used a paraffin lamp. There was no electricity. We bought paraffin from a local shop about 1km away.

We had no regular meals as there was work to do in the fields and in the house. We had a cow, which had to be fed and milked and then taken on the rope for grazing for a couple of hours on a grassed road dividing the neighbours' and our property.

Our main food was bread and milk, and *Maleszki* and milk mixture – a thick, sweet corn flour cooked like porridge. Occasionally, we had scrambled eggs. Sometimes on Sunday, we had meat for dinner, but not very often. When there was not much work in the field, my mother sometimes made *Pierogi* (similar to English pasties but boiled in water), sometimes pancakes, very often *kasza* or *pencaki* made out of pearl barley (which can be found in Britain in tins of Scotch broth). When we had surplus milk, my mother used to take it to village centrifuge, where the amount was recorded. She would get paid according to the quality and amount of milk delivered.

In front of the house there was an orchard with many trees, mainly plums and cherries, later some apples. Beyond the fruit trees was a sizeable vegetable field where we use to grow swedes, cabbage, carrots, outdoor cucumbers, tomatoes and so on. Further up still, on one side, was sweetcorn, wheat, corn, oats, barley, *tatarka*. The other side was designated for grass for the cow, for winter feed.

Many households had their own flour-grinding gadgets, called *Zarna*, a short table holding two grinding stones operated by hand. It was hard work.

Our neighbour, Hieronim Guzik built his own windmill which saved a lot of time and hard work for the neighbourhood. He took a small percentage of what he was grinding for payment. Many grew flax and made their own linen cloth, mainly for shirts.

I remember my grandfather sat on the *Kadziel* (spinning threads). My pal's father was a shoemaker. Another neighbour, Gladysz made wheels for horsedrawn wagons, so we had most of the trades locally.

4

Troublesome Times

I was about 2½ years old when my mother took me with her to the field where she was working. Being very busy, she had not noticed that I had wandered off. There was a panic. My mother and neighbours were looking for me amongst the corn, which was high. Eventually they found me with a woman from the next village about 1km away. For the moment the worry was over.

Winter came and our home was cold; there were no floorboards yet, and the frost seemed to have gone right through the walls. I became ill and the doctor said that I wouldn't make it to 4 years old. I survived the winter, and all was well until my mother sent me to the shop about half a mile away to get some flour. She gave me 5 groszy for sweets. When I came out of the shop, I spotted some kids sitting by the pond. One of them was the shopkeeper's son, who pinched my arm as I was going into the shop. He asked me for some sweets, but I would not give him any, so he pushed me into the pond and the kids ran away. Somehow, I swam towards the middle.

I remember praying to my guardian angel, then I screamed. Marsyia Szmyd, whose pond it was, looked through the window and ran quickly to her shed, where men were threshing corn. The three of them held hands as a human chain and reached me and pulled me out of the pond. Then Marysia laid me on the ground and pressed my stomach. Water was spewing out of my mouth and nose. Someone ran to get my mother, and she came with a blanket. She wrapped me up in it and carried me home. That was a very close shave. It was a deep pond. This was in the summer of 1926/1927.

The next spring, I got another soaking when I pushed some floating ice with a stick, and it slipped with me on the end of it. I fell into the icy water, but this time I got out myself.

That summer I was in more trouble.

My two pals, Janek and Staszek Dygutowicz, and I climbed a very tall cherry tree to get some cherries. As the best cherries were near the top, I climbed after them. On the way down, the tree trunk between the sets of branches was very smooth. I was half-way down the smooth part when I suddenly froze. I could not move. My pals who were lower down the tree ran off, but must have alerted someone because neighbours brought pillows and feather mattresses to put around the tree in case I fell off. Someone brought a long ladder and they got to me in the nick of time. Another few seconds and I would have fallen off, because my arms were going numb.

Winter came with a vengeance that year. The first snow fell at the end of October, which lasted for a few days, but the second fall of snow stayed down until the end of April. When we woke up in the morning, every metal fitting inside the bedroom was covered in white frost. The locks were frozen solid, so my mother used some paraffin to defrost them. The first job was to light the fire. The windows were so frozen on the inside that you could not see what the weather was like outside. I would blow on the glass until the ice melted enough to make a peephole. The snowdrifts were up to 14ft high in places, and when the snow hardened, I could climb half-way up the roof.

Beside the range we had a cast iron stove which heated the room quickly. The wood was brought to the house by horsedrawn wagons from the Carpathian Mountains driven by Rusinov Lemkow. Sometimes we would buy coal from Andrzej Cluzik, who used to work on the railway. He had a free supply of coal. One night, my mother closed the shutters of the chimney too much and we were overcome by fumes. My mother and I were very ill. We were vomiting, and if it wasn't for my grandfather who had been sleeping in the other room, we would have been dead.

My mother and my grandfather taught me the alphabet and how to sign my name before I went to school. I went to school when I was 7 years of age. There were five of us going together: Staszek Cuzik, Staszek and Janek Dygutowicz, my cousin, Tadek Gromek, and myself.

The school was situated in the centre of the village on the main road from Krosno to Dukla, 2.5 to 3km from where we lived. We used to wait for one another and went together. About half-way to school there was a bridge across the Lubatowka River. A large tree had fallen across the river and had been flattened, making a 12in-wide bridge with a handrail on one side. It was the longer way to school, but we use to go that way now and again. The road to school was along the river and when the ice was thick enough in the winter, we used to slide home on the ice.

On the other side of the road from school was the *Dom Gminny* or Community House, where the village committee held their meetings. There was also a dance hall, stage, shop, clock and tower with a bell, which was rung on special occasions like a death or fire, and joyous occasions like Easter Sunday. Not many households had a clock so people would go there to find out the time. The head of the village, or *Soltys*, was elected by the villagers. Every household had to give at least a day's work for free to repair the roads or any other work that was required.

People were very helpful to one another without asking for payment. If there was an imminent thunderstorm or hailstones or any other crisis, the neighbours came and helped to gather the crops in or assist in any way possible. We never locked the doors during the day, except when going out to the village or to town, but we locked them at night. I remember my grandmother's sister's house next to ours. There were icons of various saints all around the walls. There must have been at least thirty of them. They were approx. 2ft by 18in in size. The last thing I heard from Halina was that Hania Ziemianska had them.

5

About My School

The headmaster, Mr Golda, and his wife were the teachers residing on the premises, with another lady teacher helping out a few times a week. A priest also visited for one hour a week to teach us religion. Mrs Golda taught Class 1 and 2, and Mr. Golda Class 3 and 4. We started lessons at 9am and finished at 2pm, with two 10-minute breaks. I liked it in school. We were given homework on the first day, which kept us busy after school.

My pal's father, Hieronim Guzik was an excellent carpenter, cabinet maker, coffin maker – he made windows, doors and anything out of wood. When winter came, he made me a pair of skis. That's when I started skiing. It was a really great pleasure skiing down long hills and over jumps.

6

Illness

My mother became very ill with inflammation of the throat. She could not swallow and had a very high temperature. The neighbours thought she would die. My uncle Antoni came from the other end of Poland (Grodno), and all our relations and neighbours gathered around. Then my mother said, with great effort, 'If any of you do any harm to my Staszek, I will come back from the other world for revenge.'

My aunt Jozia made her as comfortable as she could. The doctor placed two leeches on each side of her neck. After they had enough blood, they dropped off. Jozia gave her warm lemon tea to try to swallow, and a little later Mother said, with much joy, 'It's gone.' I did not realize how close I was to becoming an orphan. Thank God she recovered.

During the school holidays, I became ill, probably with flu. When I felt a bit better, I went to see my cousin Tadek, who was holding a grazing cow on a rope. I sat down on the grass for a while, and I started to feel dizzy, so I got up and started to head towards my home. I was about halfway, I felt faint and went into the shade. The next thing I remember, there were people standing over me. I had passed out.

I don't know how long I was unconscious for; it felt like a second. I must have been very ill because my mother got the doctor to see me, and having the doctor was a last resort. I must have been close to death because I heard angels singing in the sky and they were shining through the clouds. Then I heard my mother calling my name. The doctor gave me some large pills which seemed to ferment in my stomach like Alka-Seltzer.

Gradually I recovered, but because my father died of TB, the doctors predicted that I would live for no longer than fourteen years. I had already passed the four-year and seven-year deadlines from previous illnesses, but it made me a depressed young lad. However, they were wrong.

One time, we had heavy rain and the River Lubatowka overflowed, leaving a small island on the bend. On the way from school, a few of us went by the river. Most of them could swim. I was afraid but they persuaded me to swim to the island with their help. Then they left me there, pretending that they had gone home. I thought they had, so after a while I decided to swim and made it back to the bank. From then on, I gained confidence and in a short time I could swim very well.

As my father died due to ill health caused by his time in Russia, my mother was granted a small monthly pension, which caused a lot of jealousy as money was very hard to come by. There was no work there and the only people who had money were those who had relatives in the USA, who sent them dollars. We were much better off now and my mother bought nice furniture and some nice clothes for me and herself. Life was much easier now.

7

Mugging

One day as I was on my way from school, two brothers named Kubal stopped me, demanding money. I gave them the 5 groszy I had on me (roughly the equivalent of a penny). Then they warned me not to tell anyone or they would beat me up. They also demanded that I bring some more the next day. I was afraid as I had no father to protect me, so I made excuses to my mother that I needed money for school. Eventually, I had to tell the truth. My mother took me to their parents and, from then on, I had no more trouble.

Coming home from school one afternoon through a stubble field, I spotted a little rat-like animal. I gave chase. It did not run very fast, and then it stopped and looked at me as if to say, what have I done, why are you chasing me? I stepped on it and killed it. That is on my conscience to this day. I can't forgive myself.

It must have been the year of 1933. There was a typhus epidemic in the area and most surrounding villages. In our village, Glowienka, fourteen people died including two very talented young brothers, Janek and Bronek Guzik (Szymunow). We were afraid to sit too close to one another in case they had lice which transmitted the disease.

The year of 1935 was an eventful one. On 12 May, Poland's leader, Marshal Pilsudski, died. The country was in mourning. He was the one who freed us from Austrian, Prussian and Russian occupation, which had lasted for over 120 years. A solemn song was composed in his honour which all the schools were singing. I remember some of it:

To nie prawda ze ciebe juz niema,
To nie prawda ze jestes juz w grobie,
Chociaz placze dzis cala polska ziemia,
Cala polska ziemia w zalobie,

Ty odsedlez po czymch nadludzkich,
Nie zwyciezy juz ciebie bol, zaden
Ukochany Marszalku Pilsudski
My zyjacy twoim pujiziem sladem
To nie prawda ze odszedles na wieki

This roughly translates as:

It's not true that you are gone,
It's not true that you are already in your grave,
Although the whole Polish land is crying today,
The whole Polish land in mourning,
You leave after being superhuman,
Pain will not beat you anymore, none,
Beloved Marshal Pilsudski,
We are living in the footsteps of your sacrifice,
It's not true that you are gone forever

I cannot remember anymore.

At the end of July and the beginning of August, we experienced a terrible hurricane. Very dark clouds were gathering in the west and there was an ominous rumbling noise emanating from them. My grandfather thought it was a hailstorm, but when it came closer it was frightening. The colour of the sky was purple-black, the low clouds were hanging like ripped rags, with thunder and lightning every few seconds. Then the winds came up.

My mother and grandfather were holding pillows against the windows in case the wind pushed them in, while praying at the same time. I was too frightened to pray. There was a terrible rumbling and creaking sound, and seventy roof tiles came tumbling down. It was very frightening. Then the hurricane blew over into the neighbour's field about 100ft away. Two large poplar trees were snapped about 20ft from the ground. They were around 2ft in diameter. Some oak trees about 15in in diameter were snapped about 12ft from the ground. In the neighbour's front garden, on the other side of our house, two large apple trees were torn out at their roots. The wind must have been worse north of Krosno, as a small forest of oak trees was flattened.

8

New School

That year, I went to a higher school in Krosnoby called Cwiczeniowka.
The teaching staff were all professors:

Polish language – Professor Zych
History – Professor ZIeziewcz
Geography – Professor Luciow
Mathematics – Professor Jablonski
Arts – Professor Probulski
Gymnastics and sport – Professor Patla
Religion – Dr Fuksa
Music – Professor Siemaszkiewicz
Once a week, we also had Dr Lorence.

Now, I will name some of the students I remember: Two Jewish brothers,
Hersz and Samuel Weinstein. Also, Friefeld, Luft, Halaman, Eisenberg
and Pasternak. From the German community (who came from Romania),
there were Burger, Knoll, Strhl, Klimowicz and Stepniewsk. Other students
included Stanoch, Gacek, Wajda, Kubit, Popowicz. I can't remember all
of them.

My mother's most favourite shop was a Jewish shop by the name of
Fessell. They had everything in their shop, all jumbled up, but they were
very obliging. I tasted my first orange from their shop. Once they came
to us (*na goscine*, for hospitality) for tea. My mother bought an *Otomana*,
a lovely settee, and two nice pictures, one of St Anthony and the other of
St Teresa. As the only child and a boy, I was spoilt and most things I asked
for my mother gave me (within reason). Once, however, I wanted to see
a cartoon film of two characters, Pat and Patachon, but my mother did
not have the 15 groszy for the entrance fee. I wanted to see it so much.
Perhaps that's why I like cartoon films now.

9

Krosno, an Industrial Town

In Krosno, we had two glass factories, one rubber factory, *Gumownia*, two linen factories, and a large engineering works, TPG. In the district, there were many petro-oil towers, *Szyby*. In town, there were three churches. The main one was *Fara*, as well as a church of the Franciscan Fathers, and one for the Capuchin Fathers. The churches always had a full congregation. There was also a synagogue.

Krosno also had three high schools, *Cwiczeniówka*, including a *Gimnazium* (or Gymnasium, a kind of selective entry secondary school similar to a grammar school) called Nicholas Copernicus, as well as a private *Gymnazium*.

10

Pigeon Obsession

While visiting my distant cousin, Janek Markiewicz, he gave me a pair of pigeons. Not satisfied with the pair, I bought some more, and in short time I had about twenty birds. I used to watch them fly before I went to school which sometimes made me late.

Time and again, Mother scolded me for being late for school and neglecting my homework due to looking after my pigeons. One day she said, 'If you don't get to school on time, when you get home, your birds will be gone.'

I was late again. On returning from school, I looked at the chopping block and to my horror there were feathers where their heads had been chopped off. I never kept pigeons again.

Around that time, a compulsory purchase order was made for twenty houses and a brickyard to make room for a large aerodrome between Tloki and Krosno, about 2km away. When they were demolishing the brickyard, my aunt Jozia and her husband obtained permission to take the bricks away. They transported the bricks by wheelbarrow until they had enough to build their own house. Theirs was the first brick-built house in Tloki. The other houses were built from wood with thatched roofs. Both of them worked extremely hard until eventually the house was complete.

The work on the airfield started, and men and companies arrived from all over Poland and many of the local men found work. Most local households took in lodgers, which improved their financial position and therefore their standard of living – especially those with horses, as they were transporting materials such as sand from the Jasiolka River and goods from the railway station. We had lodgers from Warsaw who came to do special jobs.

Open air dances were organized and, with them, drinking and fighting. They were called *Festyny*. They usually started at 6pm and finished at 6am. There were many fights, with knives and coshes frequently deployed. The law was lenient. Three-to-six months' suspended sentence for a stabbing, for coshing, less.

Policemen were a rare sight. They wore dark blue uniforms and carried rifles. There were now two dance halls in the village. One in the centre and the other recently built for Stanislaw Gladysz (whose son Edek had pushed me in the pond). A few of us young lads used to look through the window to watch the dancing and listen to the music. The popular dances then were the tango, foxtrot, slow fox and polka.

One day, some Jewish people came to buy our cow. My mother brought her out from the stall for them to inspect. One of them hit the cow with a horsewhip, the cow bolted, dragging my mother against the line post, where there were thick nails for tying the clothesline to the post, ripping the back part of her hand down to the bone. They turned their horsedrawn wagon around and drove away laughing.

Later in the winter, other Jewish people came to buy the cow and this time they bought it. Shortly after, there was a terrible blizzard, and we heard bellowing outside the window. The frightened cow had broken free and came home. I'll never forget the fear in her eyes. I begged my mother to keep her, but she needed the money, so the cow had to go.

In 1937, my pal Staszek Guzik and I sat exams for high school (*Gimnazium*). I passed but my pal failed. There was an enormous amount of jealousy. During school holidays, Staszek, his two brothers and their cousin, Zygmunt, started throwing stones at my cousin, Tadek, the two Dygutowiscz brothers and myself. Zygmunt ran towards us, threw his stone and when he turned back, one of his gang threw his stone at us, but instead hit him on the nose causing a deep cut.

Of course I got the blame. My mother took me over to explain that it wasn't me who hit him, but his father slapped me in the face with such a force that I saw stars. Then he hit me again. (Later, he chopped his fingers off on the circular saw, on the hand that hit me with.)

My mother bought me a smart uniform and cap. The uniform was compulsory, and had an emblem on the sleeve with the number 557 on it.

The subjects taught in the *Gimnazium* were more advanced than in the *Cwiczeniowka*, with the addition of Latin and German languages. The maths teacher was a horrible man with a German name (I heard later that he was a German spy). The German language teacher, Mrs Sobkowa, was nice. From the first day, she spoke to us in German. Our religion teacher was KS (Father) Dr Matyka. I cannot remember the names of the other professors.

By now, the construction work on the airfield was well advanced and we had a few new students who came from northwest Poland with their airmen fathers. I remember only two. One of them was a short, dark-haired chap by the name of Czarnecki, and the other was tall, blond-haired chap named Klosin. I believe their fathers were high-ranking officers in the air force.

In March 1939, the Germans invaded Czechoslovakia and there was talk of war.

In our village an ex-army sergeant named Stefanik organized the young people and lectured us on warfare, defence and what to do in the case of a gas attack. We were marching with wooden rifles and singing patriotic army songs. At the airfield there were many twin-winged training planes flying every day.

When taking off, they flew directly over the village houses so we did not get much peace, but no one complained as they were defending our land. Later, single-wing fighter planes (*Mysliwce*) arrived, and single-engine light bombers (*Karas*), one twin-engine, *Los*, and a twin-engine, *Zubr*. There was a large white plane with three engines which made a very high-pitched noise when taking off.

11

Preparation for the German Invasion

Many people began converting their cellars to air raid shelters. Others were digging shelters in their gardens, making sure that they were airtight in case of a gas attack. Meanwhile, there were several crashes of the *Karas* bombers under suspicious circumstances. My two pals and I witnessed one only 200yd away. The engine just stopped, and the plane crashed in a cornfield.

We were first at the crash site. There was a strong smell of petrol. The pilot in front was hanging half-way outside the plane. The pilot at the rear of the plane was in a seated position but he wasn't moving. It was a long time before any attempt was made to save them. With today's aircraft technology, they would almost certainly have survived.

Six of these planes crashed. They discovered later that it was sabotage. They found powdered sugar in the fuel. I don't know if they found the culprit.

One day on the way home from college, an accident occurred which nearly cost me my sight. Three of us were running, pushing each other and messing about, when one of them, Urbanek, found a cluster of dried thistle heads and threw it at me, which went straight in my eye, causing severe pain. I could not see or open my eye. My other pal, Beben, helped me to get home. Mother took me to see one of our distant relatives, Marysia Markiewicz, who was known for her skill at curing eye problems. She put some thick liquid in a glass, steeped a feather in it, and put it under my eyelid. It eased the pain temporarily but for several days I could not bring anything even close to my eye without excruciating pain.

The threat of invasion was increasing. Two anti-aircraft guns and a searchlight were installed within the First Group complex. There were three groups. The headquarters were part of the First Group, along with the airmen's quarters and three aeroplane hangars. The Second Group had two hangars where they kept trainer aircraft. The Third Group had one hangar and only a few aeroplanes.

The groups were deployed in a triangle about 1km apart. The Third Group was clearly visible from our window. The airmen were very well looked after. They had smart uniforms and excellent food. Many of the civilians who worked there were allowed to eat the leftover food.

One of our lodgers from Rymanow went home for the weekend and failed to return. When we asked his friend about him, he said, 'You won't see him again. He had a nervous breakdown and attacked his father with an open razor.'

When his father shouted, 'Son you wouldn't!', he stopped then cut his own throat twice. It was most upsetting, as he was such a nice quiet man.

12

Patriotic Propaganda

'We are not going to part with one inch of our soil,' said our Foreign Minister, Józef Beck, in early May 1939. On posters, there were squadrons of planes defending our land. For us youngsters, it was all very impressive. Meanwhile, in August that year, the German Foreign Minister, Joachim von Ribbentrop went to Moscow to make a pact with his Soviet counterpart, Vyacheslav Molotov. I remember part of a song which ridiculed Ribbentrop and Molotov. '*Ribbentrop z czerwona, szmata wona szmata wona szmata A my sobie gwizdrzem nato gwizdrzem nato hej*'. (This roughly translates as 'Ribbentrop with the red rag out, and we whistle then, hey.')

One night, I clearly remember seeing large columns of red light moving from north to west. It must have been the Northern Lights. The dogs were howling, and people were frightened. Frequently at that time, we could hear a sound like thunder from a southwesterly direction, although there were no clouds. The old soldiers in the village told us that it was heavy artillery on the Czech border. Some nights we could hear an aeroplane flying overhead but it did not sound like any of ours. Rumours were rife about border skirmishes and that many of our soldiers had been killed.

Espionage was rife; one servant of the high-ranking air force officers said to her friend, 'My boss is going daft. He opens the oven and talks to it.' (Possibly a radio?)

There was an old custom from the Middle Ages called *Sobotki*. On 24 June (St John's Day), we ran with lit torches made of rags soaked in oil. There was an abundance of oil in one of the local wells.

My cousin, Jozef Kubit, arrived home after many years in France He was a communist and a non-believer in the Catholic faith. People were aghast when he worked in the fields on a Sunday. He was a seaman in the French merchant navy before he came home. People still made jokes despite the serious situation. One about two Jews: '*Przyezedl Jojne I mowil ze bedzie wojna ale przyszedl Srul i mowil ze niema kul.*' ('Jojne came and said that there would be a war, but Srul came and said that there were no bullets.')

Two of my pals lived very close to Group Three. Sometimes, one of them would scribble strange words around the place. Words like Russia and some others, which didn't mean anything to us. He was also trying to teach us a new ball game, *Palant*. It was similar to cricket. I did not realize until much later that an English spy could have been living with his family.

It was getting near to the time to go back to college, then on 1 September 1939, I was asleep in the loft on nice dry hay. My mother came up into the loft and started shaking me, calling, 'Stazek, Stazek the war is on.'

I jumped up quick and ran down. There was a terrible roar of aeroplanes and exploding bombs and machine-gun fire. When I looked through the window, the middle of the hangar door of Group Three was ripped off and the *Dorniers* were still strafing. There were small heaps of manure on the field ready for the women to fork it over the ground so that it could be ploughed in. I don't know what the Germans thought they were as they kept strafing it. When they flew off, we came out to look at the damage.

My pals' father, Mr Dygutowicz lit up his pipe then someone shouted, 'Gas!'

Everybody dived into their cellars. After a while, it was realized that perhaps it was the smell of the match when he lit his pipe. When we looked towards Group Two, smoke was pouring out of the roof of the hangar, where there were about sixty training aircraft. They were completely destroyed.

The bombers did not attack the First Group complex and about half an hour after the raid, a single *Dornier* flew over, probably to photograph the extent of the damage. One of our fighters took off to engage the *Dornier* but it accelerated and flew west at speed. For us youngsters it was an exciting time, but for our parents who remembered the First World War, it was frightening. We did not realize what was to come.

There were unexploded bombs all over the place. Due to the bombers flying very low, they had failed to detonate. Five bombs were found at a road junction 200yd from our house and only 20yd from the nearest homes. Later, the bombs were collected by some Jewish people.

On the first day at 3pm, six *Heinkel* bombers flew over, dropping bombs on the Krosno main road bridge. They missed the bridge and then flew over to bomb the airfield. The two Dygutowicz brothers and I ran to the fields and lay in a sweetcorn patch out of sight. As the bombers approached the airfield, they released their bombs right above us. We thought it was the end as they came whistling down but, of course, they went forward and scored a direct hit on the anti-aircraft machine-gun positions near the Second Group hangar. We don't know how many people were killed. The air raid sirens were sounding day and night: one long blast for approaching planes and three short blasts for all clear.

The weather was warm and sunny. My mother and I went to the village. When we left, my grandfather was sitting on the step outside the house. On our return, we noticed something was wrong because my mother's sister's husband was carrying water into the house from the well. He was a very unstable man, and people were afraid of him. On one occasion, he locked himself and his dog in the shed and slowly killed her with a stick. We could hear the poor dog crying and yelping. Another time, he beat and starved his horse.

At that time, I suspected him of killing my grandfather, but it was never investigated or proved. His version was that Grandfather got up off the step when the air raid siren sounded and, going into the house, was found slumped by the door. That was on 5 September 1939.

On 8 September, a small group of us followed the horsedrawn hearse with the coffin to the cemetery in Krosno. On the way home when nearing our village, we heard the rumble of many aeroplanes. I looked up and it sent a shiver through me. Glinting in the sun were over fifty *Heinkels* and *Dorniers*.

I said to my cousin Tadek, 'Quick, let's run by the river as when the bombs explode, either in the river or on the ground, the splinters will overshoot us if we are on the slope of the bank.'

As we reached the river, the first twelve bombs impacted about 50yd away. We were bouncing up and down as the bombs exploded.

The air raid lasted for more than an hour. There was strafing and bombing. The rubber factory was ablaze and a thick, black pall of smoke went hundreds of feet into the air. They also bombed the linen works and the TFG engineering works as well. It was very frightening. I had just turned 15. On the way home after the raid, I was thinking, what is going to happen in five years, twenty-five years, fifty years?

The future now looked very uncertain and bleak. My pal's mother was working in the field when a spotter plane dropped three small bombs and injured her neck. Thankfully, not seriously. The five bombs which were lying at the road junction were playthings for the neighbour, Steliga's two sons, 7 and 8 years of age. They jumped on the bombs, hit them with sticks and rolled them. The bombs were 4–5ft long. Our hearts sank when the remaining six *Karas* bombers flew away over the Odrzykon Mountains. We felt abandoned. News was circulating that our soldiers were being slaughtered on the front line. We could hear big guns in the distance, with machine gun and rifle fire near to us and, of course, *Heinkels* flying over, then the sound of exploding bombs. Directly over us, spotter planes were flying low.

13

The Germans Had Landed

One morning, several fighter planes flew very low over our homes and landed on the airfield, making a lot of whistling sounds. Shortly after, a few *Dorniers* and three-engine transport planes followed. There was much activity during the night. They had very bright lights, and more planes were landing making those eerie noises. The fighter planes were *Messerschmidt* Me 109s.

I have to go back a week or ten days.

There was a rumour that the Germans were taking young men, forcing them into the army, and sending them straight to the front. Many of us young people and some ex-army men, including Szelc, who had been a prisoner of war in Russia with my father, all started marching east away from the invading Germans.

After ten miles or so, Szelc said to me and his two sons, 'Let's go back. What will be will be, and the Germans can go faster than us. Your mother will be worried about you.'

I hesitated, but he insisted that he owed it to my father to look after me. We came back. My mother was very pleased, although I was prepared to do anything for my country. Die if necessary. I was very patriotic.

After two or three days, a few smart German airmen called at my pal Dygutowicz's house saying, *'Guten tag, haben sie eier, haben sie butter?'* ('Good day, do you have eggs, do you have butter?')

They gave the Germans some eggs and butter in exchange for some *kolnisch wasser* (*Eau de Cologne*), some Juno Rund German cigarettes and razor blades.

Aeroplanes were taking off and landing continuously and lorries started bringing supplies. They all had the letters 'WL' on the back of them. To this day, I don't know what it stood for.* I could not comprehend how someone could come and take what is yours and there was nothing anyone could do about it. Meanwhile, there was panic buying, and goods were disappearing from the shops. Everything was increasing in price almost daily. Anyone with savings was worse off now as the money was almost worthless. A quart of butter, which cost 2 zloty today, was 6 zloty the next, and 10 zloty the day after that – and so on.

---

* WL likely denoted the Wehrmacht Luftwaffe, the German Air Force.

14

Russia Invades

News came that Russia had attacked Poland (17 September 1939) and had taken thousands of men from the retreating Polish army as prisoners. That was terrible news. It seemed all hope was lost. The Germans were already well established and started constructing new roads and buildings, bringing their own civilian companies, first Via Nova then Escania, and an assortment of other construction companies.*

---

* The exact names of these companies remembered by Stan have not been verified, though various private companies were utilized by Organization Todt during the war.

15

Uncle Antoni Arrives

One night in late autumn, a knock on the door. It was Uncle Antoni escaping with his life from the part of Poland now occupied by the Russians. Even before the war, he was attacked by Minsk Radio for organizing an anti-communist show in the Grodno area. He was warned that the NKVD (*Narodnyy Komissariat Vnutrennikh Del* or People's Commissariat for Internal Affairs – the Russian secret police and forerunner of the KGB) were asking for him. So, in the night, he decided to risk the Germans rather than the Russians. He had grown a nice beard, and the Russians still respected the Jews, so he did not have much problem moving from place to place. However, when he crossed to Poland, occupied by the Germans, it was a different matter. He was stopped by the German guards and asked, '*Bist du ein Jude?*' (Are you a Jew?) Naturally my uncle replied, '*Nein*' (no), then shaved his beard as soon as he could.

Uncle Antoni was my mother's brother. During the First World War, he was awarded the *Krzyż Virtuti Militari* (Cross of Military Virtue) for attacking a heavy machine-gun position with his platoon, capturing it and routing a battalion of Bolsheviks. He was given 40 hectares of land in northeast Poland for his achievement. He retired from the army with the rank of captain and took a teaching job. He was also the editor of the local newspaper. He left his wife with some Jewish people who had converted to the Catholic religion. At the time, his daughter Jolana was 5 years old, and his son Juliusz 2½. He was known as the 'Walking Encyclopedia'. He had a phenomenal memory.

For the moment the Germans didn't bother us. They only came for butter or for eggs. The shops had shortages of many things like needles, cotton, salt, sugar and there was no money. I said that I would not work for the Germans, so for the time being we had a discussion with my uncle on various subjects, then he taught me to play chess, which consumed most of our time. We made our own chess set from bits of wood. Gradually, various intellectuals started to visit him including doctors, professors, teachers and other acquaintances. He passed on a great deal of knowledge to me, and I had great respect for him.

The Germans ordered that all radios and cameras must be handed in, so news was scarce as there was only the German news, which only told you what they wanted you to hear. The Battle of Britain was being fought, and our hearts sank at the losses endured by the British Royal Navy that year. We were hoping that the British navy would defeat the German navy in a few weeks. We were also sure that the Germans would not cross the French Maginot Line. It was disappointment after disappointment. However, life had to go on.

Although the 1939–1940 winter was very hard, we still had plenty of food, including potatoes, swedes, cabbage, beetroot, sweetcorn, wheat, oats, barley, *tatarka* and beans. The grains were taken to the windmill for milling. We had to wait a few days for it as many people took their grains there.

16

We Were Arrested

My mother, her sister Jozia, and I went to the airbase to try to sell aunt Jozia's goose. I went with them as I knew some German, which I was taught in college. Jozia needed money for needles and cotton as she was doing a lot of sewing. The Germans arrested us and kept us for 5 hours. Eventually they let us go, minus the goose and no money. Things became desperate without money. There were items we needed.

Lodging in a house nearby was a man from Silesia, a *Volkdeutsche* (Nazi German terminology for people whose language and culture had German origins but who did not hold German citizenship), who had a small contract at the airbase. There was a lot of building in progress, and he had the flooring contract. Reluctantly, I got a job helping the floor layers and after a week I earned a few zloty to buy necessities. Later, they started building nearer our home and some more Silesian *Volkdeutsche* who spoke Polish came to work there. They were treated as second class citizens. The job was alright, and the Meister (Master) was a decent man. He didn't shout at me or ask me to work harder.

After these buildings were completed, we were transferred to the First Group where Jan Pawlak was in charge. A very decent man. Our job was to demolish some sheds and level the ground. I remember some of their names: Dziugan, Delimata, Gosztyla, Kaminski and two Zubal brothers. The man in charge of the site was an Austrian named Steiger. As I was wheeling a barrow load of earth, he came past me and whacked me across the back with a cane. It hurt really bad as I was only wearing a thin shirt. That was for no reason. He had high boots and was tapping them with the cane. I did not say anything in case I got another whacking.

After we levelled it, they dug a huge hole about 300ft long, 50ft wide and 30ft deep. They welded up a huge tank, put it in the hole, covered it with earth and planted fast growing trees over it. That was the benzene storage tank for the Luftwaffe.

Three of us were then transferred to another site, but this time it was night work. They were digging another big hole, leaving a square piece of ground in the middle at the original ground level and a trench cut through it.

The man in charge was a monster. The work was very hard, and we were not allowed to rest, not even for a few seconds. I was so exhausted that I went into the trench for a few seconds rest, hoping he wouldn't see me. After about half a minute, he found me and shouted at me. The earth was taken away by a small locomotive pulling a line of small wagons. He was running back and forth, coupling and uncoupling these wagons. We nicknamed him 'Spider' because of his bowlegs. One night was a jolly night. As he was waiting to couple up the wagons, one of them got uncoupled and rolled downhill smashing both his legs. We were overjoyed.

The main construction work was taken over by Escania. They wore khaki uniforms, and they did all the dirty jobs. They built a couple of sheds on stilts where they had their drinks. For a while, we were allowed to go there and buy drinks, but that didn't last long. They drank a lot, and didn't bother visiting the toilet. They urinated where they sat.

17

Changing the Job

It must have been late in the summer of 1940 when two aircraft manufacturing firms arrived in Krosno: Deutsche Luft Hansa and Juno. They set up in the First Group on the airbase, dividing a huge hall down the centre with a fence. One side was occupied by Deutsche Luft Hansa and the other by Juno. They needed workers, so four of us went for the job. After the interview, we all got the jobs. Working conditions were much better as most of the work was inside. We didn't have to worry about the rain and the cold, and the premises were heated. We were given square tags with a Luft Hansa symbol on it (a bird) and a number. My number was 15. The man in charge of us was a Polish-speaking German, Karl. He organized the layout of the workshop. Masses of wooden crates arrived, and our job was to push them on rollers to different parts of the workshop.

Work benches were lined up on one side of the fence with Juno on the other side. There were a few small adjoining rooms where drilling machines of various sizes and lathes were installed. One small room was allocated as *Washerei* (washery) where oily parts of the aircraft engines were cleaned with benzene, kept in a container similar in size to fish and chip shop frying equipment. Wire brushes and rags were used for cleaning the oily parts and a warm air hose used to dry them. After some time, when we had settled into the job, Fritz Powell from East Prussia became our *Meister* or boss.

Also, there in our section, were Otto, Klaus, Helmut and Erik. The *Obermeister* (Senior Master) was Herr Runge. In the office was Herr (Mr) Hahn and his secretary, a Polish woman, Quiqueres. The *Obermeister* didn't bother us much, unlike the German workers.

Deutsche Luft Hansa were reconditioning engines from BMW transport planes (known locally as flying coffins) and Bramo engines.

Juno were reconditioning engines from *Junkers* Ju 88s and *Stukas* Ju 87s. Our job was to clean the pistons with benzene and sandpaper, with a small wire brush attached to a drilling machine for the holes. Kurik from Borbka heated the piston on an electric element, brushed a solution of white powder mixed with methylated spirit and hit it several times with a rubber mallet. If hairline cracks appeared on the bridge of the piston, it was scrapped (*shrot*); if not, it was fitted with new piston rings and re-used.

Every one of us had to have an *Ausweis*, an official document to prove who we were, which we had to show to the guards on the gate. Sometimes, we were searched going in and coming out of the premises.

The BMW engines were star, rotary engines with twelve cylinders and the pistons were approximately 6in in diameter. The transport plane had three such engines. Special trolleys were used to securely move the engines around the workshop. After assembly, they were fixed to a frame in the third hangar, then run at various speeds for four hours.

Occasionally of an evening, we would go to the pictures (*kino*). Always, before the film started, we had to watch *Die Deutsche Wochenshau* (The German Weekly Review propaganda newsreel), events from the past week, mainly from the battlefront and their successes in the air and sea. Every day at the airbase, they would march and sing songs, mainly aimed against England. Some of the words I remember:

Wenn wir fafren, wenn wir fahren, wenn wir fahren gegen Engeland.
(When we drive, when we drive, against England)

Another:

Wir marshieren, wir marshieren, wir marshieren gegen Engeland
(We march, we march, we march against England)

Also:

Bomben, bomben, bomben nach Engeland
(Bombs, bombs, bombs to England)

There were other songs, not about war: *Sommer, Sonne, Erika und das einst Veronika* (the theme tune of a 1939 German feature film of the same name) and *Eili eilu ha ha ha.*

England must have been a real thorn in their sides.

One day, we knew that someone important was due because everything was spruced up outside the hangars. Many *Junkers* Ju 88 twin-engine dive bombers and Me 109 fighters were parked in such a perfect line that looking at them side on you could only see one plane.

Two of us and Otto were pushing an engine, which was ready for testing, to the hangar. At a distance of 60 to 80yd, the airmen assembled forming a square. In the centre was Hitler talking to them, gesticulating with his hands.

Otto said, 'It's the Fuhrer.'

That was the first time I had seen Hitler.

Every morning at the gate, they raised the *Hakenkreuz* or swastika flag, always facing east, and sounded a bugle.

We had separate toilets, *Damen* (ladies) and *Herren* (gentlemen), but there were special ones with the sign '*Nur fur Deutsche*' (only for Germans). The Germans were not allowed to fraternize with us, but when Fritz's wife came to visit him from East Prussia he introduced her to us. She was very pretty.

After a while, five high-ranking officers walked through the workshop. One of them was a General Jodl. They looked down at their feet but did not bother to look at us. One of the Germans was a very nasty character. His name was Vogl. He was a member of the SA (*Sturm Abteilung* or Brown Shirt) Party.

Food, although intermittent, was usually soup from their kitchens, which was either yellow or brown. Not sure what was in it. One of our men performed a trick we didn't think was possible. He put a 4in nail up his nose so only the nail head was showing.

18

The Persecution of the Jews

The Germans demanded that the Jews wore white armbands on which was the Jewish Star. They were forced to do the dirtiest and most dangerous jobs, like collecting unexploded bombs. In Krosno, there was a notorious Assistant Chief of Gestapo by the name of Becker. We were totally outraged when a Jewish shopkeeper located in the square (Rynek) opened his shop three minutes before the official opening time (I think it was 6am). Becker came over to him, pointed at his watch and shot him.

This put fear not only amongst the Jews, but amongst all of us.

19

Ghetto

The ghetto consisted of four or five houses. They sectioned off one street from the Rynek side where the Franciscan Fathers church stood, then another street on the Ul. Krakowska (Krakow Street) side, surrounded the streets with barbed wire, and put all the local Jews there – around 4,000 people. I don't know what happened to the Franciscan Fathers, but I can guess what happened to the Jews.

In our village we had two Jewish families, old Szmul, his wife, Sara, and his two sons, Icek and Josek, who lived in the house next door. One day, they were all taken somewhere and we never saw them again.

Coming home from work we saw some beautiful Jewish girls on the airfield, sweeping the runway. After a few days, they were gone. We had this terrible feeling that they had been transported somewhere, but there was nothing we could do. At that time, we still did not realize what was happening. Rumours were that they were taken to a forced labour camp and their property confiscated, but there were also rumours that they had been taken to a concentration camp and gassed. It was hard to believe that the Germans could do such a thing.

It looked like it was going to be a hard winter. It was getting very cold. My cousin Tadek Gromek was an apprentice to a tailor, a job he hated, as in the first year of his apprenticeship, he was asked to do all sorts of household chores like lighting the fire, bringing in the water from the well, sweeping the floors and running errands. One morning he didn't get up for work, so his father said, 'What's this Tadek, don't you feel well?'

Tadek said, 'I'm not going anymore.'

His father hit him a few times, so he got dressed and went. Evening came but Tadek didn't come home. They thought he had gone to visit his uncle or his grandfather. His father was now panicking. He walked over to the uncle and then the grandfather but no Tadek. Eventually, he went to the *Arbeitsamt* (employment office) and they told him that he had volunteered to work in Germany, and had already gone. His father caught up with him in Krakov, but he wouldn't come back.

20

Forced Out of Their Homes

Shortly after occupying Poland, a cavalcade of lorries with hundreds of soldiers arrived in Wielkopolska (Greater Poland, a region in the centre-west). Their method was to knock on people's doors at 6am, giving the occupants 3 minutes to get what they could and *Raus* (get out) – they had to get on the lorries which took them all over Poland. They dumped them on the heads of various villages, who were told to do what they want with them. Glowienka was allocated eight people. The leader (*Soltys*) of our village had to find places for them somewhere without causing a lot of hardship. The emptied homes were occupied by the Germans.

The Germans were now tightening the regulations. Each village had to deliver a quantity of grain, potatoes and eggs, while every cow, horse and pig had to be registered, with a numbered tag attached to each animal's ear. We were not allowed to have any of our own meat – only what was allocated to the shops, which was mainly the guts, lungs and other offal rejected by the Germans.

21

Was It Human Flesh?

On one occasion, a plentiful supply of sausages appeared in the butchers' shops. People were buying lots of them. We had some but there was a suspicion that whatever was in these sausages, it certainly wasn't beef or pork, and it wasn't rabbit, chicken, goose, duck, or turkey.

What was it?

It tasted sweet and some of them oozed a silky-matter-like liquid. It made us feel very sick.

22

The Arrests Started

Josef Warunek, an old bachelor, and his sister went in their horsedrawn wagon to the market in Rymanow. On the way, a Gestapo car pulled alongside the wagon and Josef was told to get off the wagon and get in the car. Fortunately, his sister managed to handle the wagon and arrived home safe. About a week later, she got a little parcel with his ashes inside, for which she had to pay 2 zloty. He was completely innocent, not involved with any political parties, had never been in the army. The only possible reason was that he was well dressed. The school (*Szkole Powszechna*) situated in the centre of town was taken over by the Wehrmacht. Not far from it was a bookshop belonging to a syndicate of several professors. They supplied schools with books and stationery. On one day, the professor of art, Probulski, and professor of music came to the bookshop. There were other people in the shop.

Professor Probulski made a remark, something like, 'The bloody Germans.' A man standing behind them called a guard from outside the occupied school and arrested them. A few days later, they died in a concentration camp. The art professor was a brilliant man. Now, most of the teachers, professors, ex-army, navy or air force personnel were in hiding.

One early morning, my mother and I were up and dressed while my uncle was still in bed. I looked out of the window to see uniformed Germans approaching our house in a battle formation. They knocked hard on the door and walked in and immediately asked for Antoni Patla.

My uncle said, 'That's me.'

The officer started shining a torch in my uncle's eyes and asked him, 'What rank were you in the army?'

My uncle said, 'Sergeant'.

He asked a few more questions, then they left. Apparently, the Ukrainian headmaster in our school reported my uncle. He wanted to curry favour with the Germans; his desire was to be a *Volksdeutscher* (an ethnic German who lived outside Germany), claiming that he was a German descendent, and that his name was Golda from 'Gold'. He was unsuccessful.

We did have some German collaborators and Gestapo informers. One of them was my ex-school mate, Popowicz. His father was a policeman before the war, and he remained so with the Germans. His son was executed by one of our Resistance units after it was discovered that he was a Gestapo informer. I believe that his father was also eliminated. At least six students from our *Gimnazium* were murdered by the Gestapo, not counting the Jewish students, including two lovely, handsome boys, the Magura brothers. One of them was our scout troop leader before the war.

The Germans forced the Jews to sing a song:

> *Marszalek Smigly Rydz,*
> *Nie nauczyl nas nic*
> *A nasz hitler zloty*
> *Uczyl nas roboty*

It roughly translates as: 'Marshal Rydz-Smigly talked in front of strangers but didn't teach them anything, but their Golden Hitler taught them how to work'.*

More horror news was circulating. When the Germans were loading Jewish families on to the wagons, any babies were grabbed by the legs and their heads smashed against the side of the wagon and thrown in. Becker was bragging that he had personally shot 3,000 Jews. Everybody was afraid to talk in front of strangers in case there was an informer present and, even in front of people that you knew, nothing offensive was said in case they were arrested and tortured. No one can guarantee that they will not break down under torture.

---

* Edward Smigly-Rydz was the Marshal of Poland, and Commander-in-Chief on the eve of war, who fled to Romania in September 1939 when Poland fell. From here, he supported the Polish Resistance, and later returned to Poland to fight. He died in 1941.

During the late autumn and winter, there wasn't much work to do except feed, milk and clean our one cow, so we had plenty of time to play chess. Dr Mercik would often visit for a game. At first, I couldn't win a game, but later, he had a job to win one. I was improving all the time. Many strangers used to come and discuss the news and politics, which they had heard from someone who had a hidden radio. Sometimes, they would ask my mother and me to leave the room (probably as a safeguard, in case we were arrested and talked under torture). I noticed on one occasion when a couple of strangers arrived that they were armed with pistols. It was exciting. My uncle Antoni demanded that I not mention it to anyone. I knew better than to say anything about it.

At that time, my uncle went missing for a few days. I found out later that he had stayed in a secret room in Hieronim Guzik's house. He was writing and editing a news bulletin, *OSA*, later *REDUTA*. Someone had a radio receiver, and any news was circulated amongst safe, trustworthy readers.

23

Bombs, Bombs, Bombs

December 1940. Lorry after lorry, day and night, were bringing boxes of various sizes which were unloaded around the outskirts of the airfield. We didn't know what they contained until after Christmas. Tractors were pulling two or three sledges. On each one of them a huge bomb, sky blue in colour. It was mentioned in the press that they were being stored safely away from the English long-range bombers. However, we knew different. They were preparing for war against Russia.

The stacks of bombs grew rapidly around the airfield and when they reached about 20ft high, they were covered with tarpaulins. The stack of bombs nearest to our house was only approximately 200ft away. (Very worrying.) The whole airfield was fenced off. We were quite concerned in case the Russians attacked first and dropped their bombs on the airfield. We would be blown to smithereens. They kept on piling them up, day and night.

At the beginning of May 1941, squadrons of brand-new Ju 88 twin-engine *Junkers* dive bombers started flying in, three at a time. Eventually, there were sixty to eighty Ju 88s, six *Dorniers,* a few BMW transport planes and a few *Messerschmidt* Me 109 fighters. On 15 or 16 June, as we were going home from work, we noticed a stack of bombs near each plane. It was then obvious that the German attack on the Soviet Union was imminent.

Every night there was a lot of activity on the airfield. Then on 22 June at 3am, my aunt Jozia's husband knocked the window, shouting, 'Anna, Anna, get up they are flying east'. It's only 25–30km to the San River, and beyond that, the Russians. They were taking off, one by one. Most of us who lived near the airfield were ready to get away as far as we could, just in case the Russians attacked and blew up the huge stores of bombs.

My mother went to my father's relatives. I went to my violin teacher, approximately 4km away. We climbed the hill to the fields, where we had an excellent view. It was a still and beautiful morning. We could hear the explosions in the distance then, at 6am, forty-three Me 109 fighters in one huge squadron took off from Krosno-Moderowka airfield, heading east. There was great excitement. At last, the two monsters had started fighting each other and there was hope that they would eliminate each other.

The signal to attack was given by searchlights on the border simultaneously lighting up the sky, so I was told. The Junkers were flying back and forth all day, re-arming and re-fuelling. We stayed there until the afternoon, just in case the Russians attacked, but then we went home. I saw some of the bombers coming in damaged. A couple of them flew in on one engine, one had the tail shot off. One came in to land at high speed and landed on the main road, the other side of the airfield. Something black fell out of the plane.

24

Treachery from Moscow

'*Zdrada ze strony Moskwy*' ('Treachery from Moscow') were the headlines in the newspaper. It was music to our ears. Now the danger of Russian retaliation was almost nil. The bombers were making round trips constantly, and the stacks of bombs were shrinking rapidly.

The German army was advancing 100km per day at first, taking thousands of prisoners. They met very little resistance against their superior armament and disciplined troops. Headlines in the press, on placards and in the cinema stated '*DEUTSCHES SIEG AN ALLEN FRONTEN*' ('Germany wins on all fronts'). In the cinemas, the *Deutsche Wocheshau* (Nazi propaganda newsreel) showed the sinking of British ships and the smashing of the Russian army. I remember when the headlines in the newspaper read 'HOOD' – they had sunk the pride of the British fleet, the battleship HMS *Hood*.*

Things weren't quite as we expected. The Germans were getting it all their own way so far. We expected the British navy to smash the German navy in a few weeks but that didn't happen. German U-boats were sinking the British fleet. Their *Heinkels* sank many ships in Scapa Flow. They said that nothing could touch them, and it certainly looked that way.

Meanwhile, the Germans demanded more and more food, like grain, potatoes and cattle. There wasn't much left. Another hard winter was approaching, and we had very little food. This was what was left after sowing: some potatoes, swedes, beans and sweetcorn. The Germans took the rest. We were hungry. Our main nourishment was milk from our one

---

* The battlecruiser HMS *Hood* was sunk in the Denmark Strait by the German navy (Kriegsmarine) on 24 May 1941.

cow. When I came home from work, my mother gave me whatever she could find and when I asked, 'Where is your meal?', she said that she had already eaten hers, but I knew that she hadn't. I was weak and hungry, and while I was cleaning the pistons I was dozing off.

25

Arrested on the Way to Church

One Sunday, four of us went to church. We were not far from the church when a Wehrmacht lieutenant stopped us and ordered, '*Kom mit mir.*' ('Come with me'.)

Stan Guzik hesitated, and he was brutally pushed into the snow. We did not know where he was taking us. Thoughts were flashing through my mind. Why were we being arrested? Are they taking us forcibly to work in Germany, or jail, or a concentration camp? We did not know. When we arrived near the courthouse, there were three lorries full of men.

My mind was a little easier when I spotted some shovels inside the lorry. They probably wanted us for snow clearing. I was right. We moved off and drove about 5km towards Miejsce Piastowe. We stopped, were told to get a shovel and get out. There were many Jews already clearing the snow. They had been there since 5am. Some of them had frostbite. One of the men had frostbite in his ear. Half of it had turned white. Another man had the first two joints on his index finger frostbitten. There were many more with frostbite, but they had to keep working.

There were huge snow drifts on the main road which we had to clear. Later, a massive snow plough arrived. It had two steering wheels and was moving huge chunks of snow. We then cleared what the snow plough had left behind. At 4pm, the kitchen arrived, and they gave us hot, thick soup full of beans. It went down well. The Jews did not get any. It was a relief when they told us that we could go home. The Jews had to go back to their ghetto. They had nothing to eat all day. We were always hungry, and the winter was very severe, so we felt the cold even more.

The German army was advancing towards the Black Sea, in the south towards Moscow and Leningrad in the north. They were recruiting men to work in the occupied territory. Two brothers, Jozek and Franek Kubal volunteered, as things were very bad here. At least they thought that they would get some food. They were lucky. They were taken to Sevastopol and Symferopol on the Black Sea where it was nice and warm. After three months they came home on leave well fed, suntanned and with plenty of money. They were well looked after. They went back after three weeks.

26

Congregation of Monsters

As we were going to work one sunny morning, it was August or September, we saw standing on the south side of the First Group, approximately 100yd from the road and about the same distance from the hangar, two large four-engine planes. As we were nearing the gate, the four of us – Staszek and Janek Dygutowicz, Kazek Kubit and I – saw what only a few other people could have seen.

Outside the nearest plane stood Hitler, Mussolini, Herman Goering, Count Ciano, Joseph Goebbels and a few other high-ranking officers. Inside the plane I could see a few more people. One of them was wearing a trilby and thick-rimmed glasses. They were all going to fly over the Russian Front. I had not seen this type of plane before, and I have seen many different kinds including a five-engine plane with twin fuselages. I believe they were *Focke-Wulfs*. My pals who are still alive will probably remember this day.

Later that autumn, part of Deutsche Luft Hansa moved to the Second Group with some of the workers, including myself. My other mates were left in the First Group. They employed more people, and one of them was my old school mate, Jozef Pudlo. There was a shortage of almost everything and for trouser material we used sackcloth. Even that was scarce. The problem was that every sack was stamped with the German eagle holding a ringed swastika in its talons. One of the men wore the swastika on his backside, which offended the Germans, so he had it dyed. He was a lathe operator. One day he took some cutters without permission and was searched on the way out. They found them, and contacted the Gestapo, who arrested him. His mother came and begged the director on her knees, trying to kiss his hand, to let him go free. They told her he must go to work in Germany. After two days he was gone, and we did not hear from him again.

Two of the workers, brothers Stefan and Staszek Kopac, came from the village of Suchodol. Both were well educated. The elder brother, Stefan was a very talented violinist. Their father was a director of the agricultural college in that village.

27

Gestapo Execution

One evening, Stefan and his friend killed a calf and put the veal into milk churns topped up with milk, and drove a horsedrawn wagon to Krosno to sell it. On the way, the Gestapo stopped them, made them empty the milk out and found the veal. They shot his friend on the spot and took Stefan to Gestapo headquarters. His father went there to plead for his son's life. They told him to bring 50,000 zloty by 7pm the next day and they would see what they could do. His father tried frantically to raise the money. There were no telephones or transport he could use to get the large sum needed. So, he borrowed it from friends and relatives and wherever he could, and he did manage to raise the 50,000 zloty. The Gestapo took the money and still shot his son. He was a handsome fellow.

At work one day, all the controllers and the Director *Obermeister* gathered around one engine, puzzled how a bird's head had found its way into the sump. Even the typist Frau Kasperek came to have a look. She was a brilliant typist. I have never seen anyone type so fast.

Just before Christmas 1942, part of the hangar was cleared and strange-shaped objects started to be brought in. These looked like portable toilets, with a large dish which had an antenna in the centre. The dish could move up and down, but the whole apparatus could revolve through 180 degrees. They told us to be extremely careful with the tube-shaped object between the dish and the main part of the apparatus, and that it cost 400 Deutsche marks. Inside there were hundreds of different wires. Only two of our men were working on the wiring.

It was one lunchtime, and we were outside, when a twin engine *Messerschmidt* Me 110 took off, and as it circled, it exploded in the air. Now, the Germans besides working during the day, had to do fire watching during the night as the long-range British Lancasters were reaching further into occupied territory. I don't know whether the British had any bases in Russia as they appeared to be flying from east to west. Their engines made a different sound to the German aeroplanes. We heard that they had bombed Vienna. It was music to our ears.

28

A Warning to the Girls

The Resistance warned women and girls not to fraternize with the Germans. If they continued, their hair was shaved off and if that did not stop them, they had an arrow tattooed from their navel down, with the words *Nur Fur Deutschen* (only for Germans), which would lessen their chances of marriage in the future.

29

My First Errands for the *Związek Walki Zbrojnej* (ZWZ – Union of Armed Struggle)

One day, my uncle had two visitors. One of them was 'Orski', and the other 'Bazant'. They had pistols tucked into their belts and did not bother to hide them from me. Orski said to me, 'Take this bit of paper, go to this address, and say a password. Show him your bit of paper and he should have one to match it.'

There was a very strict code of silence: Do not talk to anyone whatsoever of what was said or who is who. I was very enthusiastic about it all; anything I could do for my country. They trusted me. I was useful to them.

Meanwhile, as the front went further east, Deutsche Luft Hansa moved out to somewhere nearer the front line. We were getting news that the British aircraft were inflicting heavy damage to German factories and power stations. A lot of it was exaggerated, but we loved it.

30

My New Name

Eventually, Orski came to see my uncle and said to me 'Staszek, we cannot call you by your name, choose yourself a pseudonym.' I hesitated for a while, then said, '*Jakis Zwierz*' (some animal). 'That's it', he said, '*Zwierz*.' So, from then on I was only known as Zwierz. These pseudonyms were given in case any of us were caught by the Gestapo. We could not divulge anybody's name under torture, as we did not know their real names.

Our home was a safe house, pseudonym *Malwa* (Debris). Very often, important people would visit the house, stay the night and leave the next day with one of the Resistance members. I heard that they went to Hungary and then on to the West. One night, Orski said to me, 'Stay outside and be very alert, there is someone very important in the house.'

It was Whitsun and the custom in our part of Poland was to decorate the outside of the house with tree branches. I sat on a bench hidden behind one of the branches. It was warm and my eyes were closing, but I managed to stay alert all night.

Another safe house was about half a mile away, pseudonym *Zdechlina* (Carcass or Carrion). It was in a very strategic position with a clear view overlooking the airbase. It belonged to a widow, Henjarka, and her two sons. They were very poor. The floor was flattened earth. Her older son, Edek had tuberculosis.

There was a safe house in Bobrka, pseudonym *Bagno* (bog or swamp), and one in Leki Dukielskie, pseudonym *Kozielec* (goat). From *Zdechlina*, we could see clearly what was happening at the airbase, right under their noses. When we moved from place to place, we would go in pairs, approximately 100ft feet apart and usually at night.

31

My First Weapon

My first pistol was a small 6mm calibre, later replaced by a Winston five-shot revolver, very awkward behind the belt.* There was an acute shortage of weapons of any kind, so we had to get them wherever we could.

My first dangerous situation arose when Orski asked me to bring a rifle from Polanka village. There were two isolated houses; it was the first one on my route. The person knew that I was coming for it. I gave the password, and he invited me in. Orski assured me that there were no Germans in Szczepancowa or Zrecin, which were on the way. Orski said that there may be a few lorries passing but they shouldn't stop you. It was about an 80-minute walk from Bagno. I went there in the evening. It was early March, and I had a good idea how to camouflage the rifle. We wrapped the rifle in straw, leaving loose straw by the trigger, then cut an apple sapling with the roots at one end of the rifle and the crown at the other then tied it tightly so that it would not fall out.

I was up early the next morning walking towards my destination, but when I came to Szczepancowa, a shiver ran down my spine. It was swarming with Wehrmacht. All it needed was for one of them to come close to me and he would have noticed that it wasn't only a sapling. I had no choice but to go on, trying not to arouse suspicion. Fortunately for me, a horsedrawn wagon drove along, and the fellow asked me if I wanted a lift. He was going to Wrocanka, which was the next village on my route. It was divine providence. How easily I could have been caught. However, the mission was accomplished. Orski was very pleased with my ingenuity.

Most of us knew each other by their pseudonym, although, later, we discovered real names when in conversation. Orski was our commandant.

---

* Stan may have been thinking of a Wesson (Smith & Wesson).

His second in command was Bazant, later changed to Kar. His adjutant was Niemsta, real name Kazimierz Czlowiekowski. There were Litavor and Msciciel, the Opatiewich brothers, whose ex-army elder brother was shot in the head from behind by the Germans, but still was conscious enough to get his handkerchief out, put it against his head wound and run a few yards before collapsing. From the start there were Kruczek Mis Jastrzab, Orlik Lis, Smrek, Giewont, Natan, Aniol (Konrad Budzik) and Jasiek Z Wasami, a sketch war correspondent and photographer.

Rej Kuna, my uncle, was the editor of the underground press. Gradually, there were more and more of us, mainly the intellectuals whom the Germans were after.

When the Germans discovered the mass graves in the Forest of Katyn and published the names of the dead, my uncle cried like a baby. Some of the murdered, including General Olszyna Wilczynski, were his friends.*

Gestapo informers were eliminated first, as they posed the most danger to us.

The first one, a woman, by Orski, Bazant and Pokrzywka. She was seriously wounded.** They forced the nursing sister on duty at the hospital to take them to her room on the ground floor and shot her in bed, then jumped through the window into the night. The second person that they proved was a Gestapo informer was killed with a hammer as he was going through a hole in the fence to meet his girlfriend. He possessed two pistols, one his own and the other was Gestapo issue. It put a lot of fear into would-be informers. They knew that there was no escape from the Partisans. They would be discovered sooner or later and shot.

There was a company of *Grenzshutz* (border guards) stationed in part of Krosno. The officers' stables were about 200yd away from their quarters, but right opposite the home of one of our lady Partisan members put them under observation and their routines were timed.

---

* The Katyn Forest Massacre of 1940, in which thousands of Polish prisoners were killed, apparently by Soviet soldiers. A mass grave was uncovered by German Army in 1943, and exploited to full effect by the Nazi propaganda machine.

** Apparently, they had tried eliminate her on a previous occasion and went to finish the task. (Len Czekaj)

32

My First Real Action

'*Olejek*' (AKA Romauld Holeczek) and I were told where to meet '*Wrzos*' (Jan Barniak). Orski met us a few minutes after we arrived so as not to look conspicuous. The plan was that Olejek and I would go into the stables and call the name of the stable boy, Edward (Edek for short). Orski and Wrzos were going to cover us in case of trouble. When the officers brought their last horses and returned to the barracks, we went in and Olejek called, 'Edek, Edek'.

The German came out from behind the horse and said, '*Was woollen sie?*' (What do you want?)

I pulled out my Winston revolver and shouted, '*Hande hoch!*' (Hands up.)

The frightened German said, '*Wollensie meine tashen lampe, woollen sie meine pfeife?*' (Do you want my torch or my pipe?)

He started to step back behind the horse. I said, '*Kommen sie hier*', and pulled him back.

Olejek had already picked up the lad's pistol as he had hung it on the door while tending the horses. We warned him not to shout for help for half an hour and bolted the door from the outside. As soon as we left, he started kicking the door and shouting, '*Hilfe!*' (Help.)

Olejek and I went quickly along the River Lubatowka and the job was well done. I thought I would get the Walther pistol, but it was given to the second in command, Bazant. I thought that wasn't fair.

Around that time, the German hero was Colonel Mölders. It was claimed that he had shot down 613 Russian planes. He got killed later in a transport plane crash.

One morning when my uncle and I were home, my mother said, 'I had such a strange dream, I dreamt that a three-engine transport plane crashed behind the village of Suchodol (the next village) and seven high-ranking officers were killed.' Three days later, it happened exactly at the spot she had described, and seven high-ranking officers died.

Some of us were moved to Kozielec (Leki Dukielskie) into some houses on the outskirts of the forest. We were joined by four Russian prisoners of war, who had escaped and somehow managed to contact us. They had darker skin than us, so we had to be careful not to walk with them in the daytime. They came from the Caucasus Mountain area of Azerbaijan. They brought three rifles and an automatic submachine gun, a PPSz (the Polish designation of the Russian PPSh) with clockwork magazines holding seventy-two rounds of ammunition.

They made us feel nervous when we were all asleep (except the guard outside); one of them stayed inside on guard with the automatic weapon. We were sleeping on the floor with our clothes on, squashed tightly together like sardines, and only our shoes off. They could decide to mow us down as we slept, and there wasn't much we could have done. One of our men heard that they were planning some sort of action against us, so Orski ordered six men to take them to one of our safe places near Jacmietz with '*Drop*' in charge (I was told what had happened by Orlik, who was with the group).

On the way, they rested in a barn. Then, on a signal from Drop, they shot them. One of them, a teacher, was a very stocky man, and his whole body was covered in thick black hair, including his forehead and cheeks under his eyes; the only exception were his palms and the bottom of his feet.

He was shot four times in the head with a Luger and was screaming like a pig. Then one of our men pierced his neck with a bayonet, he grabbed it and tried to pull it out. Only when they stabbed him in the chest several times did he die. During the shooting, one of our men '*Chmiel*' was accidently shot through the knee. That was the end of his participation in active service.

Back in Glowienka, Krystyna, the beautiful 17-year-old sister of '*Grzebyk*', was working at the airbase as a waitress. She stole two Walther pistols and then braved it and stole a Bergmann machine pistol. She took it to Olejek, but he refused to accept it, so the poor girl took it back to her house and hid it in the cellar under some potatoes. The Gestapo were suspicious and tortured her, found the Bergmann then shot her. Had Olejek accepted it, she might be alive now.

Two of our men, '*Wrzos*' and '*Ziuk*', went to one of our safe houses in the village of Kopytowa. On the way they got stopped by a German patrol and asked for *Ausweis* (identification papers). Instead of them looking slowly through their pockets, they got nervous and panicked trying to get their pistols out. One German shot Wrzos with a Bergmann machine pistol and wounded Ziuk, who managed to shoot the two Germans.

According to some local people who witnessed it from their windows, he shouted to some young children to get away, pulled the pin from a hand grenade and put it to his head. We were moving from place to place, mainly at night through the forest, and knew the route by heart. On one occasion, four of us set off to go through the forest which normally took 20 minutes. After two hours we came out from where we started.

During the winter in the snow, Smrek was going from Kozielec to Bagno on the route we often used. He got lost as he was following his own footprints. The men going to the morning shift at the factory left a trail and only then did he find his way.

33

Torturing of Prisoners

After careful planning, a group of Partisans from the Jaslo region managed to release some prisoners from Jaslo jail. Orski told us that the Gestapo had stripped them naked, tied them up by their arms and legs to the wall and let Alsatian dogs savage them. They tied their arms and legs together, hung them upside down and poured water in their noses, hitting them with wooden clubs on their knees and the soles of their feet. When the Gestapo were drunk, they would make them run along the corridors and shoot at them. The prisoners were dispersed to our safe houses and tended to by doctors.

Meanwhile, at the airbase, the Germans built wooden sheds on the site where the bombs had been stored. Eight thousand Russian prisoners were housed in these sheds. Within six weeks, most of them had died from typhoid, typhus and dysentery.

34

Execution of a Forester

Four escaped Russian prisoners were hiding in a forester's house. One morning. the forester asked them to let him sow some clover as it was the right time in the season. They let him go, but instead of sowing clover, he went and reported to the Germans that there were prisoners in his house. The Germans surrounded the house, and the Russians scattered into the woods. Two of them were shot dead and one was wounded but managed to escape. The fourth prisoner escaped without a scratch. When we found out about it, a few of our men went in and hung the forester upside down in a pear tree close to the house and set fire to the building and so he fried to death.

This I was told; I did not witness it.

35

Another Action in Krosno

Our supply of boots was running low, so action was organized to obtain some from a cobbler, whose shop was on Korczynska Street, who repaired boots for the Germans. It was autumn, dark at 7pm. A horsedrawn wagon pulled up at the back of his shop. Four of us went into the shop, Msciciel and I stood guard outside. Anyone coming into the shop was let in, but no one was let out. After they had loaded the boots into a sack, and onto the wagon, I went in and tried on a pair of boots from the pile that was left on the floor. There were around ten people guarded by our men, who had entered the shop while we were there.

When I found the pair of boots that fitted, I said, 'I am leaving my old boots for Herr Becker.' (The Gestapo Monster.)

The wagon drove off, we split up, and Pokrzywka and I walked towards Kroscinko. On the main road, parallel to the one we were on, were two cars – probably the Gestapo looking for us. The cobblers' shop was about 300–400yd from the Gestapo headquarters.

I was suffering with severe indigestion, and I said to Pokrzywka, 'I need something to ease this, I can't go on.'

There was an isolated house near the roadside, so we went in. An old fellow was sitting by his stove upon which was an enamel mug filled with boiling water. We asked him if we could have some. He said, 'Of course you can.'

I drank some of the hot water and the indigestion went almost straight away. From then on, I knew a good remedy for indigestion. The problem of lack of boots was temporarily solved. However, they did not last very long as we were constantly walking through the fields and forest getting them wet and muddy. Our group was on the move most of the time, using up lots of energy.

The sweetener we had for our barley coffee was saccharine. Niemsta said to Orski, 'The boys need sugar, saccharine is no good for the heart.'

Our reconnaissance team was observing a German farm, *Lanwirtshaft* (agricultural). Seven men went in and they came out with some automatic weapons, a pig and three 100kg sacks of sugar. After that action they were very tired, so I was put on all-night guard duty, with orders to wake them if there was any sign of Germans. My observation point was a house high up on the hill. The expected German pursuit never happened.

Marching one night towards Frysztak, Chef had to answer the call of nature and was left behind. After we had walked about 3km, he caught us up and then he realized that his Walther pistol had slipped from his belt. He had to go back by himself and try and find the pistol in the pitch dark. He did find it. When we arrived at Frysztak, a courier came rushing to tell us that one of our places in Odrzykon was 'burned' (which meant betrayed) with two of our people shot dead, and that the Gestapo were very active in this area. Although very tired after our long march, we had to cautiously move out of the area. Danger was ever present, so during the day we stayed indoors out of sight so as not to endanger the people and to make sure that no informers would see us. We then moved back to our old safe places in Bobrka and Leki Dukielskie. There we stayed quiet except for reconnaissance activities.

36

Attacked by Shupo and Ukrainian Police

It was around the middle of March 1943 when we moved towards Frysztak again and occupied three houses in a cul-de-sac surrounded by hills on three sides. The morning of 19 March, St Joseph's Day, was the 'name day' of our commander Orski. In Poland, we celebrate 'name day' or *Imieniny*, instead of birthdays, a day to honour the saint with the same name.

There were about thirty of us performing the usual morning routine. Some were shaving, some were drinking coffee, and one was ill with flu. Natan, Orski and Niemsta rushed through the door and said, 'Quickly, get dressed and, one by one, run towards that ridge and start shooting.'

Lis and Pik ran out with the light machine gun, Kar had the rifle and started shooting. As we ran out, the bullets started hitting the house and the trees around us. The only route out was up the hill which was very slow due to the snow. The bullets were hitting the branches all around us.

Miraculously, no one was hit. We were now deeper into the forest, up to our waists in snow, which made the going so much harder. On the way we met a fellow with a rucksack on his back. We stopped him and searched him. He had several bottles of vodka, *Samogonka* – homemade stuff. Chef took the vodka from him, and I think he gave him some money. We all had a little drink which cheered us up. We marched a long way with few stops for rest. After about 40km we arrived at Kozielec. '*Mamuszka*', Orlik's mother, and her two daughters were already there, and our meal was cooked ready for us. They then left with Orski on a horsedrawn sledge.

Shortly after, news came from one of our contacts that one of the bigshot Germans was planning a birthday party for his daughter and that Becker would be there. Msciciel, Grot and Janczar were on guard duty outside where it was very cold and frosty. Suddenly, Grot was overcome with fear, took his boots off and started running away. Msciciel and Janczar ran after him and caught him. He was shaking violently. They managed to quieten him down. At the birthday party, the surprised Germans suddenly realized what was happening and one shouted, '*Polinishe Banditen.*' (Polish bandits.)

We pointed our pistols at them shouting, '*Hande Hoch.*' (Hands up.)

After disarming them, they were bundled into the cellars. Maszynista grabbed a woman's handbag, and it's just as well as she had a Belgian *Fabrique Nationale* or FN automatic pistol inside it, which would have been disastrous. Unfortunately, Becker was not there, which was the main object of the raid. Luckily for us, a blizzard had developed covering our footsteps in the snow. We had a good haul of weapons, food and other items.

The next night, we went back to our favourite place in Kozielec. More and more joined the Partisan troops and it was split into *Oddział Partyzancki* 11 (Partisan Unit 11 – abbreviated to OP-11.) and OP-15. Our section, OP-11, moved to the Wieczno area and OP-15 to the Iwonicz area.

At that time, large German units were combing local villages and surrounding forest looking for Partisans. We were very lucky not to be caught. Located in two large farmhouses nestling in a depression amongst the hills, the Germans never searched there. We were told that there were 5,000 Germans involved in the search.

37

Moving Farther East

When it had quietened down, we moved to Bazanowka near Jacmierz, where we stayed for a couple of weeks. For food, we had to steal a cow from a friendly farmer. All cattle had to be registered and carried a numbered tag clipped to an ear. But in the process, it was necessary to kill a lovely Alsatian guard dog. One of our men who knew the dog had to kill it, as the barking would arouse suspicion amongst the neighbouring Germans. He killed it with a spade.

Around that time, one of our boys was cleaning his pistol, and unbeknown to him, had left a bullet in the chamber. It fired while he was dismantling it, injuring his hand and singeing Msciciels's neck, while the bullet lodged itself in the wardrobe. Motto: Always treat a gun as loaded.

38

Parachute Drop

A few days later, there was a parachute drop from a British plane. We had six Sten guns, two Bren guns, several hand grenades, some green uniforms and chocolates. I had a pair of British Army officer's boots, which were the only ones in the drop. I thought that they weren't going to last long as the soles were thin with 'S'-shaped studs, but they were marvellous, really comfortable and they lasted a long time. The British hand grenades were bigger than the Polish ones. When the pin was pulled out, it had to be thrown immediately. With the Polish grenades, if the handle was held, the pin could be re-inserted for later use.

39

Concentration

There were now several hundred of us and we were split up into OP-11, OP-15 and OP-23. We were joined by four Russian paratroopers and six Jews who had survived the Holocaust. In charge of the Russians was Vasilko; I think his rank was major. He had a Luger pistol with a very long barrel. I had not seen one like that before. He also had a guitar and often strummed it, singing quietly to himself.

The Germans were retreating from the Russian Front, and we were marching towards it. We stopped in the forest to cook a meal. Chef said, 'You boys go on and I will find some mushrooms.'

We did not go far, and I was puzzled because what I thought was a freshly-cut tree stump was in fact a giant mushroom. When I brought it to the camp, they were all amazed at its size. Shech (the war correspondent) took several photographs of the giant which I held surrounded by the group.

40

Mystery of the Disappearing Jews

We moved near Zagorz, occupying several houses. Orski put Natan, Vasilko and one of the Jews on guard duty. The Jewish man was a tall, stocky fellow with big ears. When the guard was changed, the Jew did not return, and the same thing happened the next night. Another one of them did not return. One of the other Jews was concerned and asked me, 'Where are they?' I did not know but one of the fellows said that they had been moved to another platoon.

Then, they took the other three supposedly to the other platoon. I was suspicious because where Natan was, death wasn't very far away. We were joined by a few more men, but I had a suspicion that they were Ukrainian spies. They had that guilty look about them. I must mention one of them. He could grow a moustache within three days. One of the new recruits suddenly went berserk, as if possessed by the devil. His eyes went red, and he was jumping about screaming with sweat pouring from him. Someone went to get a doctor from a quiet distant village.

The doctor said, 'I'll take him home with me.'

Orski sent Natan to escort them and I don't know whether Orski gave the order to shoot them, or he shot them himself. Natan said that they had run off, but he had the doctor's watch on his wrist.

41

Ambush

One of our platoons hid in a field of potatoes by the main road lying in wait. When a column of German soldiers on foot passed them, they opened fire at close range with all they had. They killed many of them. They then retreated to the outskirts of the forest still firing. I have never heard such a concentration of fire. My pal, Msciciel, was lucky. A round from a German machine gun tore a hole in the ground, 6in from his side while he was lying down. The platoon captured six Germans, including one Frenchman who wanted to join us, and Orski agreed that the other five were left to Natan.

Natan and another man took them into the forest and shot them. The youngest was only 18 years old, and he shouted '*Heil Hitler*' before he was shot. There was no way we could let them go and we could not take them with us. Natan was an evil man who took pleasure in killing. Niemsta upset him when he told him that he probably had wristwatches from his shoulder to his wrist.

We were in a hostile terrain where most of the villagers were Ukrainian. There was one big Polish farm where we managed to get a food supply. As we were approaching the farm gate near the house, two beautiful young girls were smiling at us from an upstairs window. We were informed a few days later that the Ukrainians had murdered all their family and set fire to the house. The Ukrainians were friendly towards the Germans.

The food supply was grim. Orski sent four men to see if they could get some. All they got were a few chickens and some eggs. We were quite deep in the forest, but we always had a lookout. A few of us had German helmets which were useful to sit on when we stopped for a rest and the ground was wet. One of the men on guard duty was wearing a German helmet and he was surprised by a large German patrol of thirty men. He kept his cool. They asked him if there was any food around.

He said, '*Kommen sie mit.*' ('Come with me.')

Soon, they were surrounded with shouts of '*Hande hoch*' and they surrendered. They were told to sit in a group, then Orski told Vasilko to do what he wants with them. Vasilko and some others opened up with automatic fire and shot all but two who managed to escape.

We crossed the River San and came across a huge gun emplacement, permanently fixed pointing west. We climbed a very steep hill and had 15 minutes rest at the top. I don't know what was on top of that hill, but after those fifteen minutes, I felt as if I was just starting the march.

It was somewhere near Ustrzyki Dolne that we witnessed a big battle. Howitzers and Katyushas blasting continuously. It was a frightening sight. There were tank obstacles all along the river, pieces of railway line 3ft long, welded together in such a way that whichever position they were placed, they always stood upright. It had rained and walking through the fields and forest was exhausting. We were wet and the ground was slippery. Some of our men were so tired that they were dozing as they walked. It was pitch dark, but we were always alert. After an hour's march, we rested in a deep forest.

We were in the Zagorz area, high up overlooking the main road, when our patrol reported a large column of Germans approaching. In front were several soldiers on horseback, twenty horsedrawn wagons and a column of marching soldiers. We waited until the wagons had passed then opened fire on the marching column with whatever we had. I had a Spandau machine gun with a tracer every fifth bullet, which allowed me to see in which direction the fire was going.

We shot quite a few but then they reorganized and went on the attack with heavy machine guns and rifle fire. Then we heard the rumble of tanks advancing towards us, so we had to retreat as we only had one anti-tank weapon, a German *Pantzerfaust* (anti-tank rocket launcher). Their fire was intense. We retreated into the forest, but later our patrol reported that we were surrounded. We had to cross the main road running through the forest to get even further into it, where there were deep ravines which were inaccessible to tanks.

Quietly during the night, we got through without a shot being fired.

We came to a place called Sukowate, where there was a very large house belonging to the forester. We were waiting for the overall commander Korwin, who was coming to inspect our battle readiness. The scenery there was beautiful. Three identical large hills covered mainly with pine trees, and oak and beech trees dotted about. Some of the men went hunting wild boars. Korwin and his adjutant arrived with the news that Ukrainians had massacred men, women and children during a church service. The local school headmaster was the leader of the Ukrainian bandits and was executed by Szpagat and Natan.

42

Ukrainians Escaping the Advancing Russians

After we had left that place, we stopped to cook a meal in a forest near a woodland road. As we were settling down, a convoy of horsedrawn wagons was passing through. Orski instructed us to stop and search them. They were ordered off the wagons and to sit in groups of five. We found ex-Polish army officer sheets, blankets, cutlery and some documents.

When the Polish Army was retreating under German pressure, the Ukrainians were shooting them in the back. They must have been guilty because one of the groups split and ran. They were shot almost immediately, except one person who ran for about a kilometre and was shot as he ran. To avoid any more escapes, they were tied up with ropes found on their wagons. One of our men, Grzebyk, recognized some of them as the same people who murdered sixteen of his relatives. He got his own back, giving them a good beating with the rope. Several of our men marched them a distance away. Grzebyk, Msciciel, Orlik and the four Russians. Half an hour later, we heard automatic gun fire. They were made to dig their own graves then shot. There were more than eighty of them.

There was plenty of food, vodka and honey in their wagons. I still have a table knife that belonged to one of them.*

We had some vodka mixed with honey and it seemed to perk us up, recharging our energy. We killed a cow and were cooking it when Orski came up and said, 'Pack it in, the Germans are advancing.'

I swallowed a hot potato in a hurry and felt it burning my insides. The Germans opened up with machine-gun fire, but we retreated into the forest. Later, heading towards one of the villages, we were pursued by

---

* I remember the knife that Stan described, but I have no idea what happened to it. (Len Czekaj)

three German tanks with heavy machine-gun fire. Some of us ran up a steep hill, while others dropped down into the trench alongside the road. A German who was looking out of his tank was shot by one of our men. His helmet fell off and he fell back into the tank. Duch jumped up and dropped in a hand grenade. The other two turned around and drove off.

43

Korwin's Blunder

We went high up into the hills covered with forest. There was a clearing on one side. It was a very bad decision by Korwin to take this position. We had very little food and no water. Morale was at an all-time low. He sent a patrol for some food. Two hours later they came back with a few loaves of black bread and some eggs. He gave each of us a small piece of bread and kept the rest of it for his closest staff. We were outraged when we discovered that he had only used the egg yolks and had thrown the egg white away. We were hungry. As soon as anyone showed themselves outside of the forest, machine guns shot at us. The Germans knew we were there. We were expecting a barrage of German artillery to fire on our position at any time.

44

Rebellion

After the food being wasted even though we were starving, we started planning to depart from there. Old Stary, Msciciel, Orlik, myself and a few others, eight in all, slipped away one night and headed nearer home. I had a topographic map of the area, so we planned our route carefully, trying to avoid built-up areas as there was predominantly a Ukrainian majority in this area and they were very hostile towards us. Hungry and tired, we came down towards two farmhouses. Running down towards them, Msciciel slipped, and as he fell, his Sten gun hit the ground and fired several rounds into the air.

When we reached the farm, we were given fresh milk, plenty of bread and butter. It was bliss. The farm belonged to a Polish farmer who gave us some information on the whereabouts of the Germans and which of the villages were populated by Ukrainians. The front line wasn't far away and there was the continuous sound of heavy artillery, and German and Russian aircraft were active. We passed a house where German soldiers were sitting in the garden, they looked at us but did nothing. We walked normally not showing any signs of nervousness until we passed out of their sight, then we sped up. We were heading towards our old safe house in Bobrka (known as 'Bagno' in code).

The village of Lezany not too far away was already in Russian hands. Stary and three others split up and went in a different direction. Orlik, the two Opatkiewicz brothers and I went towards Bobrka. We were told by some people that Glowienka, Krosno and the airfield were still in German hands, but the Russians occupied the Odrzykon Mountains north of Krosno and were shelling German positions.

We hid our weapons, now that we were dispersed, waiting to see what was going to happen next. Russian planes were now more prominent than the German planes. I witnessed a Russian *Ilyushin* single-engine aeroplane attack a column of German lorries, setting them alight. It was a slow flying plane but had tremendous fire power. In Lubatowa, horses taken from the Germans were hidden in stalls. When the Germans passed nearby and the horses heard them talking German, they started neighing and the curious Germans discovered them. They shot many people. As the Germans retreated, they placed small charges on the railway lines chipping about 6in off the end. We had to take great care as there were many landmines, some so small that they would explode with the slightest touch. Stepping on one would have blown your foot off. After a week, Orski and the rest of OP-11 came to the Krosno area. He was quite cross with us for leaving by ourselves.

He said, 'You should have trusted me, I wouldn't let you down.'

He admitted that Korwin made a mistake.

He ordered us to cover all long weapons like rifles and machine guns in Vaseline and wrap them in rags and we stored them in a hideout next to my house. A hole was dug along the side of my house and two concrete pipes which had been used for water wells were positioned in the hole, covered with earth and a well camouflaged trap door was fitted, which could be opened at a moment's notice. The short weapons, pistols and hand grenades were hidden in straw in the loft. I had my Luger, and two hand grenades wrapped in oily rags.

A Russian aeroplane landed on the airfield, probably thinking it was in Russian hands. Realizing his mistake, the pilot ran to the nearest building and escaped. Anytime that the Germans tried to get near the aircraft, the Russian artillery pounded the airfield. Orski ordered our men to take the guns from the plane, which they did, and hide them in the long grass. The next night, he ordered me and two others to bring the guns to our house. It was a pitch black night, but we found the guns and the ammunition belts, and we came under heavy automatic fire. We returned fire but only took the ammunition as the large calibre guns were too heavy. Some of our lads got the guns the next night but they weren't any good, as they were fired by pulling a steel line. Much too hard to pull by hand.

Several of our group were in my house and some of the rest of the group in the house next door when fifteen Germans were slowly approaching in a battle formation. Some of our men were in the loft and some in a room with the curtains drawn. I went behind a hedge. My mother bravely came out with a bottle of *Samogonka* (homemade vodka) and offered some to the Germans. The officer in charge told my mother to drink some first, then they finished the bottle.

Except for artillery exchanges and machine-gun fire at night, there appeared to be a lull in the battle. The Russians were on the Odrzykon Mountains, and the Germans on the Carpathian Mountains, so the missiles were overshooting our location. Orski told me to stay near my home and when he needed me, he would send someone to get me. I stayed in an empty house which used to belong to my mother's parents. There was a primitive sort of bed with straw for a mattress which I slept on. I frequently went just outside the door to listen to the artillery shells whistling overhead and watch the flashes as they detonated. At one time, I saw several German cars speeding from Krosno towards Zrecin being blasted by Russian artillery. As they reached the built-up area the shelling stopped.

Stan's first Holy Communion.

Anna Czekaj, Stan's mother.

Antoni Patla, Stan's uncle.

Anna and Alojzy's wedding, 1923.

Stan (left) with an army friend in Germany.

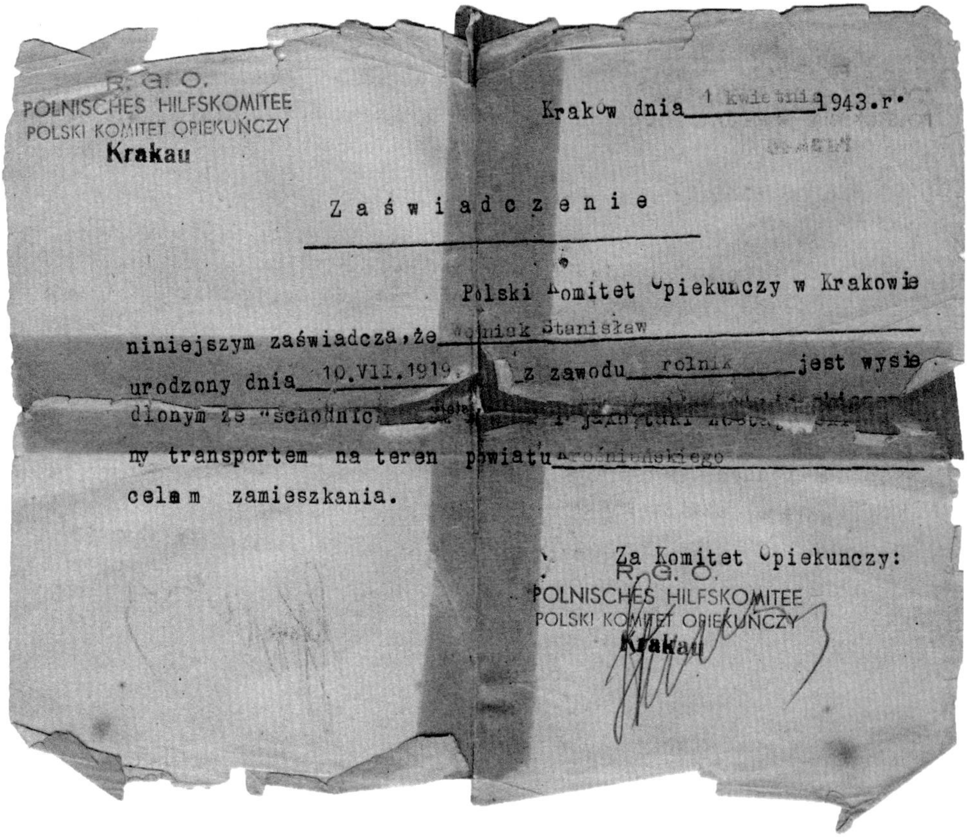

R. G. O.
POLNISCHES HILFSKOMITEE
POLSKI KOMITET OPIEKUŃCZY
Krakau

Krak°w dnia ___1 kwietnia___ 1943. r.

Z a ś w i a d c z e n i e

Polski Komitet Opiekuńczy w Krakowie

niniejszym zaświadcza, że ___Woźniak Stanisław___

urodzony dnia___10.VII.1919___ z zawodu ___rolnik___ jest wysie

dlonym ze "schodnich ____________ i jako taki został ____________

ny transportem na teren powiatu ___________________

celem zamieszkania.

Za Komitet Opiekunczy:
R. G. O.
POLNISCHES HILFSKOMITEE
POLSKI KOMITET OPIEKUŃCZY
Krakau

Stan's transit document to Krakow issued by the Polish Welfare Committee, dated 1 April 1943.

Stan's Resistance group Op-11 in action on 17 March 1944.

Stan's Resistance group in Germany. Stan is not pictured – he was most likely the person taking the photograph.

Colleagues from the Holy Cross Brigade in the American Occupied Zone, c.1945.

Stan's group at the Nuremberg Trials.

Stan, pictured second from the left, as a guard during the Nuremberg Trials.

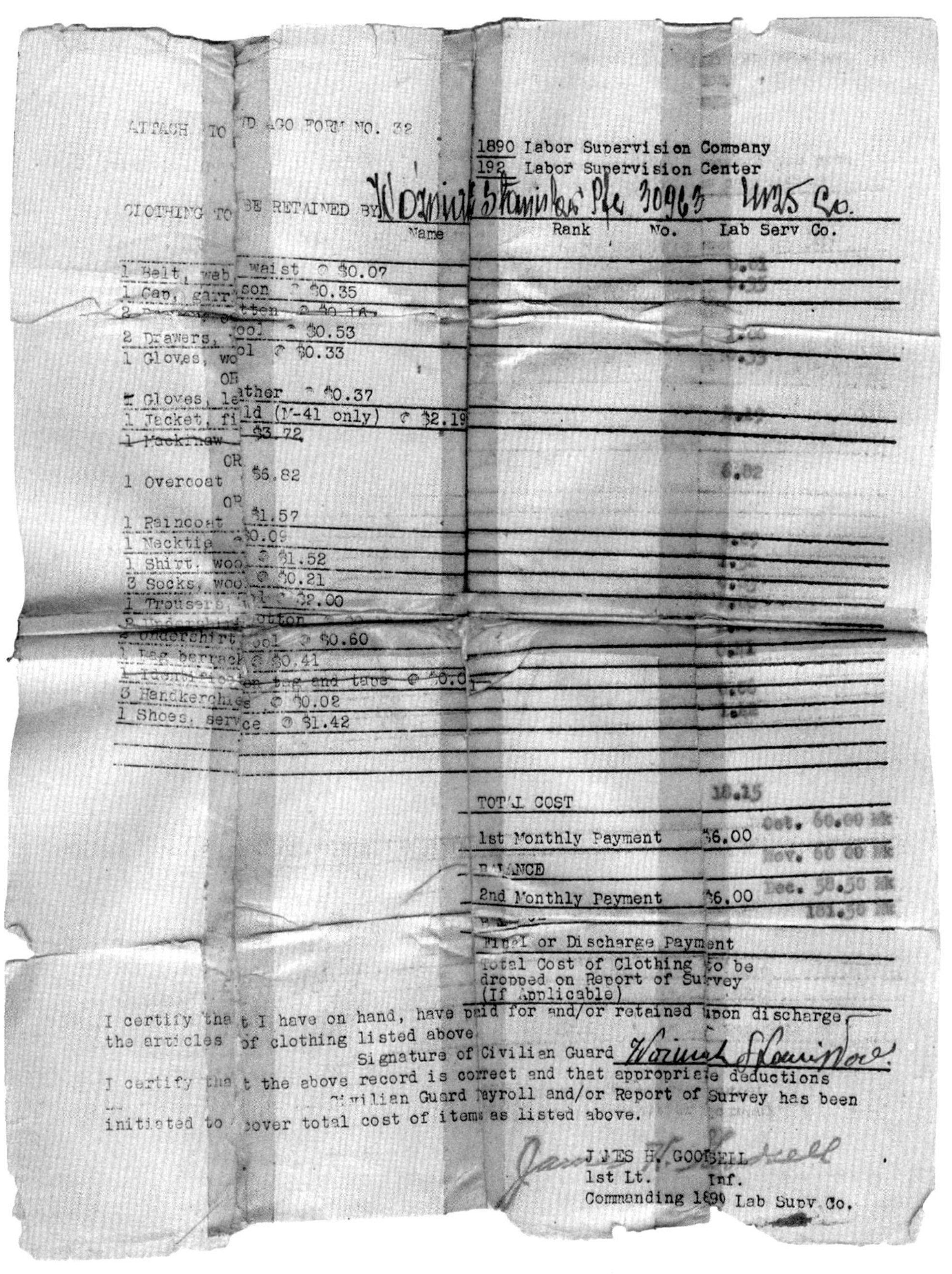

ATTACH TO WD AGO FORM NO. 32

1890 Labor Supervision Company
192 Labor Supervision Center

CLOTHING TO BE RETAINED BY _Woxxxx Stanislaus Pfc 30963 LuS Co._
                            Name   Rank   No.   Lab Serv Co.

1 Belt, web, waist @ $0.07
1 Cap, garrison @ $0.35
2 Drawers, cotton @ $0.18
2 Drawers, wool @ $0.53
1 Gloves, wool @ $0.33
        OR
1 Gloves, leather @ $0.37
1 Jacket, field (M-41 only) @ $2.19
1 Mackinaw $3.72
        OR
1 Overcoat $6.82
        OR
1 Raincoat $1.57
1 Necktie $0.09
1 Shirt, wool @ $1.52
3 Socks, wool @ $0.21
1 Trousers, wool @ $2.00
2 Undershirt, cotton
2 Undershirt, wool @ $0.60
1 Bag, barracks @ $0.41
1 Identification tag and tape @ $0.0
3 Handkerchiefs @ $0.02
1 Shoes, service @ $1.42

TOTAL COST 18.15
1st Monthly Payment $6.00   Oct. 60.00 Mk
BALANCE   Nov. 60.00 Mk
2nd Monthly Payment $6.00   Dec. 38.50 Mk
BALANCE   181.50 Mk
Final or Discharge Payment
Total Cost of Clothing to be
dropped on Report of Survey
(If Applicable)

I certify that I have on hand, have paid for and/or retained upon discharge
the articles of clothing listed above.
                    Signature of Civilian Guard _Woxxxx Stanislaus_

I certify that the above record is correct and that appropriate deductions
Civilian Guard Payroll and/or Report of Survey has been
initiated to cover total cost of items as listed above.

                                   JAMES H. GOODSELL
                              1st Lt.   Inf.
                              Commanding 1890 Lab Supv Co.

Discharge papers signed by First Lieutenant James H. Goodsell.

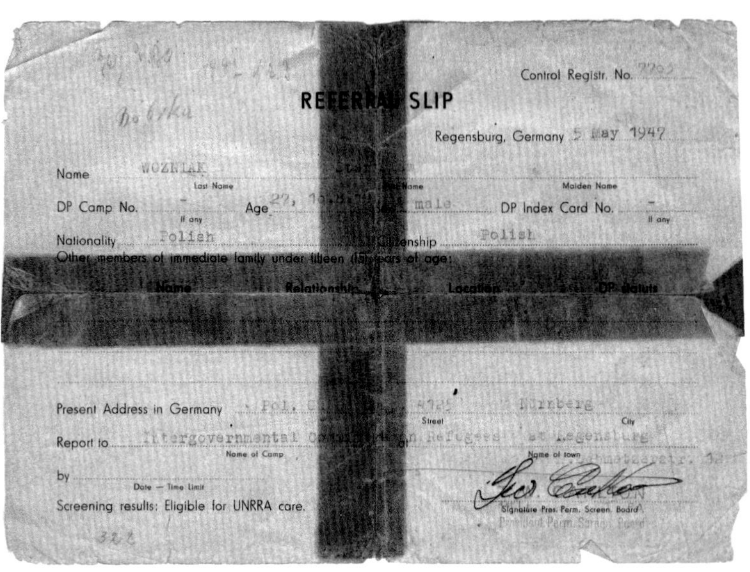

Office of the Military Governor
U. S. Zone of Germany

CERTIFICATE OF IDENTITY IN LIEU OF PASSPORT

PC 013103

1.   WOZNIAK Stanislaw
                   (name in full)

born at   Bobka   Krosno   Poland
          (town)   (district)   (country)

on 10 of 8 1919 M Polish
   (day)   (month) (year) (sex) (citizenship)

                                          intends to emigrate to

          (given & maiden name of wife, if applicable)

          England
          (country of immigration)

2. He (she) will be accompanied by   none

(List here all family members, with name,
birthplace and date, and citizenship
of each)

3. His (her) occupation is   Coal Mining

4. DESCRIPTION

Height 5 ft 9 inches

Hair brown   Eyes grey-brown

Distinguishing marks or features:

          none

5. He (she) solemnly declares that he (she) has never committed nor has he (she) been convicted of
any crime except as follows: none

6. He (she) is unable to produce birth certificates, marriage license, divorce papers and / or police
record for the following reasons: lost during the war

7. I hereby certify that the description of the person(s) whose photograph(s) is affixed hereto is correct and that he (she, they) declare(s) that the facts stated above are true.

(signature of applicant)

Signed 28 1 1948
        (day) (month) (year)

at Frankfurt a/M
                (location)

                (signature of certifying officer)

                Paul J. McCormack

          (country of immigration)

2. He (she) will be accompanied by   none

Stan's temporary passport with fake name,
dated 28 January 1948.

Staff of the Walton Park Hotel in 1949. Stan is seated on the far right with arms folded.

Stan and Nesta on their wedding day in 1951, pictured with Nesta's parents, Alberta and Ernest.

Stan and Nesta cutting their wedding cake.

Anna with Antoni and Len, c.1960.

Nesta and Anna in 1961.

Stan in 1962, aged 38.

Stan in 1968, aged 44.

KOŁO BYŁYCH ŻOŁNIERZY ARMII KRAJOWEJ

POLISH HOME ARMY EX-SERVICEMEN ASSOCIATION

42, EMPERORS GATE, LONDON, S.W. 7.

L. dz. .... 26·3·70
Our ref.

80 Horn Lane
London W.3.

Szanowny Panie Kolego!

W załączeniu przesyłam leg. Krzyża A.K.
dla: 1. Korubal Adam
2. Pikul Władysław
3. OPATKIEWICZ Marian
4. OPATKIEWICZ Waleriam
5. Widniewski Jan

Informuję jednocześnie, że proszę być ostrożnym
z wysyłaniem pocztą, gdyż ostatnio zdarzyły
mi się wypadki że listy te były skradzione
na poczcie krzyżowej. Lepiej byłoby wysłać
okazją jak ktoś jedzie do Polski lub oddać
komuś kto jest tutaj z Polski.

Z okazji świąt składam serdeczne
życzenia Zdrowych i Wesołych Świąt
Wielkiejnocy

J. Skoczymikowski.
Sekretarz Komisji Krzyża A.K.

Polish Home Army Ex-Serviceman Association document dated 26 March 1970.

Stan's medal certificate dated 27 April 1970.

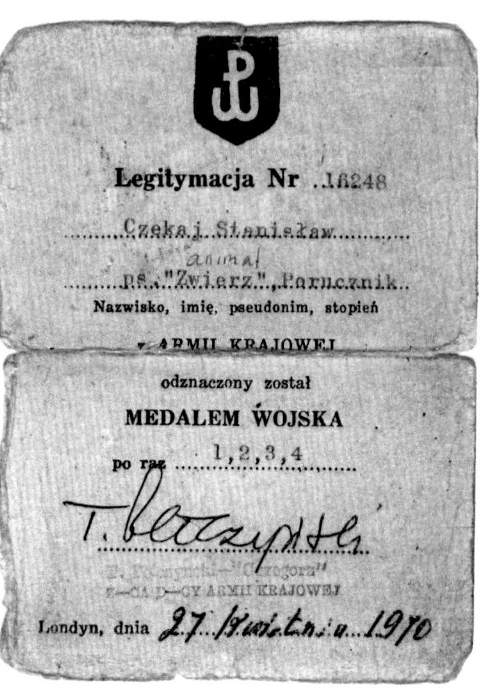

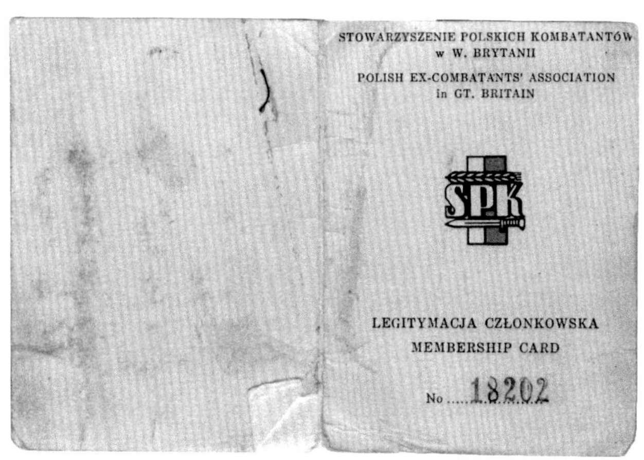

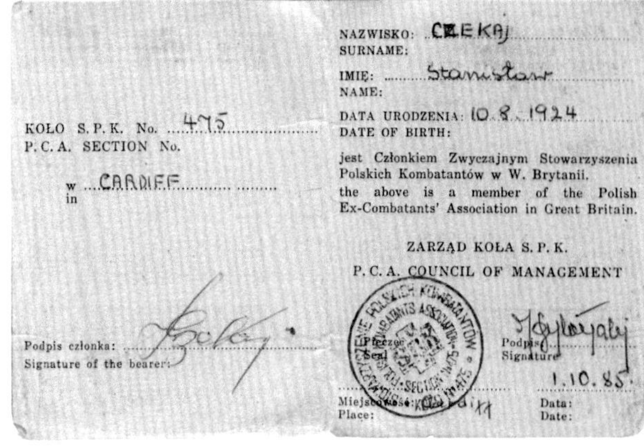

Stan's Polish Ex-Combatants' Association card dated 1 October 1985.

Stan in 1979, aged 55.

Stan in 1980, aged 56.

7.30 NESTA

8.00

8.30 I am writing this while

9.00 I can.

9.30 If something happens

10.00 to me I would like

10.30 to be buried with the

11.00 Poles and like the

11.30 writing on the Cross

12.00 or Stone to be:

12.30

1.00 STANISLAW FRANCISZEK

1.30 CZEKAJ

2.00 PSEUDO "ZWIERZ"

2.30

3.00 PARTYZANT Z.W.Z.

3.30 A.K.

4.00 ODDZIAŁ ORSKIEGO

4.30

5.00 O.P. 11 PODKARPACIE

5.30

6.00

6.30 I love you Nesta and

7.00 I love the Boys.

7.30 8/11/89

Stan's last wishes. It reads:

'Nesta, I am writing this while I can. If something happens to me I would like to be buried with the Poles and like the writing on the cross or stone to be:

    STANISLAW FRANCISZEK CZEKAJ
    PSEUDO "ZWIERZ"
    PARTYZANTZ.W.Z
    ODDZIAŁ ORSKIEGO
    OP-11 PODKARPACIE

I love you Nesta and I love the boys.

8/11/89'

45

The Russians are Coming

I had a message from Orski to go to Bagno. On the way, I saw what appeared to be six shiny humps. Two were white and the other four were brown. When I got nearer, they were six dead horses with their stomachs swollen near to bursting point.

I reached Bagno and stayed a few days with Mr and Mrs Sep. I used to work for their son, Wladek, in Deutsche Luft Hansa. His sister, Stasia, was quite sweet on me. She was a decent and pretty girl.

The Russians started their offensive with the infantry advancing and extensive artillery, tank and machine-gun fire. From the window we could see the German machine-gun position. An approaching Russian tank shot at it, a little short of target, the second shot a little too far and the third shot a direct hit. I sat opposite the window looking out. As I got up, talking, describing something, I moved one pace, and a bullet hit the spot where I had just been sitting. It hit the wall at chest height and lodged itself in the wall.

A Russian girl came into the house, shot through the ankle, took her shoes off and tended to her wound. They brought in a young Russian soldier, 21 years old, a big fellow with a shrapnel hole in his back the size of a 10p piece. He was crying for his mother all the time. A Czechoslovakian hospital was nearby but they would not admit him or treat him. Our girls bandaged his wound but that was all we could do for him.

Three cars carrying German civilians tried to escape into the forest. Shells from Russian tanks fired and exploded in front of the cars, and Russian horsemen caught up with them and they were taken prisoner. We watched this from the window as it happened.

Now, the German artillery started to shell the village of Bobrka, about a dozen at a time at short intervals. The house I was in didn't have a cellar but the one 20yd away did. Women and children were in the cellar while the men stayed in the corridor. One shell hit the corner of the house but thankfully it didn't start a fire. It was frightening. When there was a lull in the shelling, Mrs Sep went out to get a bucket of water from the well. The shelling started up again and a piece of shrapnel hit her in the neck. It left a deep flesh wound and thankfully missed her spine. There were quite a few buildings on fire including the church.

News came in that a Russian division of 8,000 men and 1,600 horses had fallen into a trap and had been slaughtered near Dukla; and worrying news that there were many fires in Glowienka, which gave me grave concern about my mother's safety. I went to have a look for myself. I walked through Szczepancowa towards Glowienka, where my house stood. I could see my home was still intact.

As I came nearer, I was shot at, so I lay down and looking toward my house, saw that Russians were there already. Half a mile to the right were the Germans. To my amazement, a horsedrawn field kitchen came right up to the front line. They were brave men. I went back to Bobrka until the Germans were routed from the Glowienka area. I finally got to my house and, to my joy, my mother was unharmed, but four houses had burned down. On returning to Bobrka, I could see a battery of eight field guns at a distance of a few hundred yards still firing towards the Carpathian Mountains.

As I walked through the fields near the village of Wrocanka, twelve Me 109 fighters flew over, followed by exploding Russian anti-aircraft fire. I was in a field with nowhere to hide so I just watched the show. Within minutes, I saw nine of the twelve aircraft shot down. As a point of interest, the German anti-aircraft shells were bigger and produced black smoke on detonation, while the Russian shells were much smaller and produced white puffs of smoke like balls of cotton wool.

News that the Germans were fighting back caused a bit of panic, but it wasn't true.

Three of us went to Zrecin, which was already overcrowded. We slept on the floor. The next day a horsedrawn wagon full of wounded Russian soldiers passed us. Some of them had bones sticking out of their limbs as four Me 109 German fighters came in low strafing along the Jasiolka River. The bullets were exploding rounds. The Germans briefly stopped their offensive but there were still a lot of artillery exchanges.

A squadron of twin-engine bombers I hadn't seen before – I think they were American planes – attacked the German positions (so they thought) and scored a direct hit on the house where the Russians had made their front line headquarters. High-ranking Russian officers killed there were buried in Zrecin, near where Msciciel and Litavor lived. I think that one of them was a general. They must still be there, unless they have been moved back to Russia. On one occasion, a Russian fighter strafed Russian anti-aircraft positions by mistake, so they turned their guns on him and shot him down.

A family of Jews were in hiding with a family in Zrecin. When the Russians got there, they complained that the family had kept them hungry. Most people were starving. The consensus of the other villagers was that they were being incredibly ungrateful when that family had risked their lives to hide them from the Germans.

46

I Became Ill

I was ill, so Orski arranged a place for me in hospital under the name Zubal, which was one of the names of the two brothers that I had worked with under Pawlak. It was extremely difficult to get a place, but Orski had donated a lot of medicine to the hospital, so it wasn't a problem for me to get a place. I was diagnosed with paratyphoid. The hospital was full and there were two patients with typhus. One was a doctor from Lwow, and his devoted wife was allowed to stay with him in the ward sleeping on a table. The other patient who had typhus recovered but went deaf. A 12-year-old lad in the next bed had malaria. One evening his temperature shot up and he was shaking like a leaf. One wealthy farmer had his leg severed clean off by a piece of shrapnel, which was 1in wide by 10in long. He was delirious, in a fever and shouting nonsense.

He said, 'I am going for a walk now', and crashed to the floor.

The sister put him back in bed, injected something into his backside and said, 'There, he will sleep now.'

He did, for good.

One of the other patients had a small shrapnel wound in his arm and occasionally his arm would jerk up violently. He had tetanus. His family came to visit him, and his daughter shook him gently and said, 'Dad, Dad', but no answer.

I said, 'He has just got back from the toilet, and he must be sleeping.'

He had died.

I was not allowed to eat any solids but only liquids, which were mainly apple and plum juice. Fortunately, I had no appetite. Towards the end of the second week, my temperature was fluctuating. It was going up and down. In the evening, over 40 degrees centigrade and, in the morning, below normal which can affect the heart. The priest who taught me at *Gimnazium*, a Dr Matyka, came to give me the last rights. He said, 'Son, you know how it is. You may not see tomorrow, so make your peace with God and pray for forgiveness of your sins.' I was very weak and on Thursday of the third week, they gave me very thin *Grysik*, semolina mixed with milk, which was the most solid food I had eaten since being admitted to hospital. Gradually I grew stronger. My dear mother came to see me every day and usually brought me something to drink.

During that time, the Germans had developed a new kind of artillery shell which once fired would explode again and push it a few more kilometres. They seemed to be exploding over the hospital. Meanwhile, Kazik ('*Lipka*' as he was known to the group) had caught paratyphoid as well, and my mother was looking after him. She did not catch the disease.

The doctor in charge of the hospital was a lovely lady, a Dr Golachowska. Most of the patients had shrapnel wounds from shells and landmines. After four weeks in hospital, I came home and for the first time in an age, I tasted wonderful crusty bread that my mother had baked, and I was recovering rapidly.

There were hordes of Russian soldiers occupying every available space they could find. They set up an office in our main room. In charge was an elderly overweight sergeant, who wore glasses. He was a nice man. He used an abacus with different coloured beads. Occupying the next house was a pleasant young soldier called Szasza, and a not-so-friendly Anton, and their lieutenant.

I asked Szasza, 'What do you think of Tovarish Stalin?'

He said, 'I would shoot him myself but how can you get near him?'

The winter was quite hard. Anton and the lieutenant drove towards the front. The next morning Szasza said, 'They are dead, a shell hit their jeep.'

The Russians had a meal twice a day which consisted of a piece of dark bread and thick bean soup. They livened it up with tins of *Swinja Tuszonka* (a canned stewed meat, especially popular in Russia). Their dishes for the soup were whatever receptacle they could find, including one soldier who ate his soup from a baby's potty. Every so often the soldiers would be given 400g of vodka, but they would drink anything with a bit of alcohol in it.

One said to my pal, 'Let me put some of your aftershave on my handkerchief.'

My pal obliged, and the soldier drank it.

47

Making Vodka

During this time, money was worthless, and the only currency was vodka. Stills mushroomed everywhere. My pal made me one out of copper sheeting, which had to be tightly panel-beaten together, as solder would melt under the high temperatures. A tight-fitting top was sealed with dough to stop any steam escaping.*

There were hundreds of soldiers and only one outside toilet by each house, so they would relieve themselves where they stood. If they slept in the loft on straw or hay, that's where their toilet was. It was impossible to walk in the dark without stepping in human excrement.

A target for the Russians was any sort of wrist or pocket watches. People would hide their watches otherwise they were forced to sell it or were dispossessed of it. I heard of an incident where there was a Russian on a train, and he saw a passenger with a smart wristwatch. He wanted to buy it.

The passenger thought to himself, 'I will give him such a high figure that he will not be able to afford it, and he won't risk robbing me in front of all these passengers.'

The soldier agreed to pay him the price but said, 'I will pay you in German money.'

There was no way out of the deal, so he agreed the sum of 6,000. When the passenger checked the money, instead of German marks, he had 6,000 American dollars!

No good-looking girl or woman was safe, they would rape them. One soldier mentioned that they went to a big house where there were many

---

* Stan made a rough sketch of the still and a recipe for making the vodka in a handwritten book, which is now with the Museum in Poland. (Len Czekaj)

women wearing hats like Napoleon. They raped all of them. Nuns. One man's wife fell for a Russian officer and rejected her husband, but after the Russians left, her grown-up children threw her out.

48

Conscription

The so-called Polish authorities conscripted young men into the army. Six schoolmates of mine were taken. After two weeks training, they sent them in front of the tanks to detonate the landmines. All were dead within a few days. Two of them were the Niezgoda brothers and a third was Jozef Zajdel. They are the only ones that I can remember.

49

I Had an Accident

On the evening of 3 January 1945, I was trying to heat up a soldering iron on a paraffin lamp, but as I did not have paraffin, I filled it with petrol. The top of the lamp was pushed on and not screwed down. When I moved the lamp, the petrol spilled onto the table and caught fire. Thinking quickly, I tried to extinguish the wick, hoping that what petrol had spilled onto the table would burn itself out.

Unfortunately, a lot of petrol had spilled onto my hands which caught alight. My hands were like two torches. I tried to quench them by putting them under my arms and pulling them out; they were still on fire. Next, between my legs; still burning. I ran into the bedroom and put my hands under a blanket and lay on them. When I pulled them out, there was no skin left on them and the pain was terrible.

The thick skin that was on the palms of my hands was hanging off in strings. The ring on my finger was starting to tighten as my hand began to swell up. My mother quickly put out the flames and ran to Staszek Dygutowicz, who came equipped with wire cutters and cut the ring from my finger. My cousin Anna was a headmistress in a very poor area, Glojsce, so she had to be a teacher, lawyer and doctor. She had some medicine for burns which she had made from the white of an egg. First, she bathed my hands in camomile flower lotion and applied the ointment, then wrapped my hands in bandages. I looked like I had boxing gloves on.

50

Russian Offensive

At 6am on 5 January 1945, the Russians opened up with everything they possessed. They concentrated 2,000 *Katyushas* on an 80km front, as well as heavy artillery. The fire was so intense that no single shot could be heard, only a continuous whooshing sound like a hurricane.

At any one time, around 100 German and Russian – mainly Russian – planes could be seen. A little ginger Russian girl fighter pilot came to us and, seeing my predicament, rolled eight cigarettes for me and put them on the edge of the table, so that I could pick them up with my mouth. I was puzzled when I saw a German plane fly past a Russian plane and not shoot at one another.

51

Raid by the NKVD

My mother and I were making vodka one evening. It was boiling well, and we had already filled five 1 litre bottles. It was 2am and there was a violent banging on the door. My mother opened the door and seven NKVD men rushed in and, immediately, the officer in charge ordered his men to search the house.*

I had a Parabellum (Luger), and two hand grenades wrapped up in oily rags on top of the pigsty with a handful of straw scattered over them. They never found them. Then they went upstairs. My mother followed them with the paraffin lamp, they didn't have torches. I had a Bergmann submachine gun hidden in the hay.

Fortunately, my mother knew where it was and so she stood on the spot where it was hidden, shining the lamp around. They pierced the straw and hay with their bayonets but failed to find anything. They came under the pretext that I had not registered for the army. Men of my age were conscripted into the Russian army.

Seeing my hands in bandages, they said, 'We will be back when you get better.'

I remembered my grandfather's words 'There is no bad that some good doesn't come out of it.' If I had not burned my hands, it most probably would have been my end.

---

* The NKVD or *Narodnyy Komissariat Vnutrennikh Del* was the Soviet secret police and the forerunner of the KGB.

52

Escape

When news reached my superiors, they acted with lightning speed and sent a horsedrawn sled and took me around 30km to Orzechowka to recover from the burns. It was a house belonging to one of our men, '*Blysk*'. In charge was Jan Thaczyk ('*Budzik*'). We were well armed with Russian PPSz automatic pistols, with a clockwork magazine holding seventy-two bullets, plus pistols and hand grenades.

Two neighbouring villages were Ukrainian and very hostile. They would steal horses and cows from Izdebki and Jasienca, two Poles. Blysk had two sisters and because of a shortage of space, I had to share a bed with one, sometimes both sisters. No sex though, as Mum slept in the bed next to us. My hands were getting better, and I was well rested.

There was a lovely looking young lady teacher at a local barn dance. Rivalry for her attention brewed between Blysk and Budzik. Although Budzik was in charge, Blysk was in his own territory and made reports to his superiors about actions he supposedly made but never happened.

53

Warning of a Raid

One day, unexpectedly, Orski, Niemsta, Natan and Lipka came and said that we must move from here as the place is going to be raided by the NKVD and *Milicja* (militia/police). They were looking for me. We stopped at another house about 2km away, and caught a Ukrainian who had just returned from Russian-occupied Germany. He was suspected of sending Poles to a concentration camp. They tied him up in a chair, asked him various questions and tortured him, especially Natan. He hit him with a stick, burned his chest and hands with a cigarette and stuck pins under his fingernails. I did not like that.

Eventually, he would not respond to questioning anymore. I heard them saying that he had been very cruel to some Poles and had sent twenty-four of them to a concentration camp. When the Russians had occupied the place in Germany where he was staying, he decided to risk coming back. Orski said, 'We cannot let him go now', and as far as I know he ordered him to be shot.

News had reached us that the NKVD had arrested many Polish Partisans and nobody knew where they were.

54

The War Wasn't Over Yet

We now had a new enemy, the Russians. Our supposed saviours turned out to be as bad an enemy as the Germans. With their total control over the Polish puppet government, the army and the *Milicja*, it was more difficult for us to operate or find hiding places, not knowing who was or wasn't friendly to the Russians. Some of our men joined the new Polish army. One of them was second in command to Orski, Kar. The Russians were always reminding us that they had freed us from the Germans (which was true) but they also started to free us from everything they could lay their hands on. All the machines from factories, railway locomotives, wagons and railway lines. Where there were two sets of tracks, they would take one up leaving a single track.

There were very many arrests in our area and in most parts of Poland. We Partisans were classed as a 'dangerous element', so they arrested many of them. Some who agreed with their politics were safe for the moment. Niemsta and Deneka got jobs in the Town Hall, but it didn't last very long.

55

Death of Orski

News reached us that Orski had been arrested in Tarnow as he was travelling by train to meet his superiors. We heard that during his interrogation, he grabbed a pistol belonging to the interrogator from the table, shot him and dived towards the window, but the guard on the door shot him with a round from his PPSz machine gun.

With Orski dead, and Kar in the army, the next highest rank in active service was Budzik, Konrad, and Jasiekz Wasami, except for the High Command at Suchodol, which were Podkowiak and Jodla. I met the boss a few times through Podkowiak, but he had more than one pseudonym. Konrad was very popular from pre-war times. He was one of the very few people who could drive a car and bus. We went almost everywhere together and most places we visited had vodka on the table. We used to drink an awful lot. I had to move from place to place as the *Milicja* were still looking for me.

56

My First Confrontation with the *Milicja*

It was on 4 March 1945, and I was going from Bobrka to Zdechlina. There was plenty of snow around and, to protect the main road from being covered in snow, fences made from tree branches were placed 30ft beyond each side of the road.

Walking down the road, I noticed two people standing in the road. I thought that they were men working on the road surface, but it was a man beating a young boy across his face. I thought that I would find out what's going on and give them a good hiding. When I got nearer, I realized that he was a *Milicjant* (militiaman or policeman), and he had a Luger in his hand. As I passed him, he put the Luger in his pocket and took out a notebook to take the boy's name. I took my gloves off, took out my pistol from behind my belt and put it in the pocket of my short coat.

I turned back as he was taking the boy's statement and shouted, '*Rece do gory!*' (Hands up.)

Instead of obeying me, he dropped the notebook and pencil and went for his gun, which left me no option but to shoot him, which I did. Three bullets in the face. Where each bullet entered, blood puffed out. He spun round three times and fell. Fearing that lorries carrying Russian soldiers would see him, I called a couple of onlookers to drag his body off the main road and place it by the fence behind the snowdrift. I put my Russian TT pistol (it was the best) behind my belt, picked up his Luger and the leather bag he was carrying, got on his bicycle and rode to Zdechlina.

I told Hejnarka, who was one of our commanders for that area, what I had done as there were spots of blood on my clothes. I took the bag and documents to Podkowiak who told me that the paperwork was summonses. Out of eighty of the summonses, sixty were for making vodka. As I found out later, he was a police commander from Dukla, named Wladyslaw Foremny. His brother-in law was in the Resistance and was not pleased about the incident. I had more enemies now. I wasn't quite sure what he might do. Podkowiak agreed with me that I had no option but to shoot. The hunt for me was now full on.

I was given an order to deliver a message in Bobrka village and, on the way, I met '*Kruczek*' (Wladislaw Pikul). He said, 'I am going to Wrocanka village (on the way to Bobrka) to my brother's Christening party, so come with me to wet the baby's head.' I said, 'OK, but only a couple of drinks.'

When we arrived, there was a 1 litre bottle of vodka on the table, so we had a couple of drinks each and the bottle was empty. There was another one, and a bit of guitar music, so I was unable to leave. I was drunk. My guardian angel was looking after me. There was a raid on Bobrka village during that night and every house was searched. Had I gone on, I would have been caught.

57

Mirage in the Snow

I have to mention a strange encounter. Walking from Bobrka towards my home, a full moon was shining on the crisp snow like it was daylight. A couple of hundred yards away, I saw a black dog running around in circles as if it was sniffing a scent. There were no houses anywhere near it. Most dogs in Poland at that time were kept for the sole purpose of guarding property. Most dogs would attack a stranger. I wasn't worried, if it attacked me, I would shoot it. As I came closer, it seemed to disappear in the snow. I looked for paw prints, but there were none. My hair stood up on end. It couldn't have run away anywhere as I could see a couple of miles in each direction.

I slept at home for a couple of nights but did not show my face outside during the day, only going out at night. I went to Zrecin village, the home of Msciciel and Litavor and stayed there a few nights. Their sister Jadwiga, Wiska for short, was 'very nice'.

While I was there during the day, four NKVD men walked in. I had some excellent photographs from the days we were in the forest wearing civilian clothes and German helmets. The picture of the giant mushroom that I had found was one of them. I just managed to hide them in the ashes under the range before they entered the room. They asked who was who, and I was introduced as the fiancé of their daughter, and they left. Some days later, they arrested Msciciel (Marian Opatkiewicz). His sister travelled all over the place enquiring as to the whereabouts of her brother, but nobody could tell her anything. She travelled to Krosno, Rzeszow, and even Krakow. After six weeks, they released him from the cellar of a house 100yd away.

There were more and more arrests. People disappearing and nobody knowing their whereabouts. My pal and neighbour, Stan Dygutowicz was arrested and he was never in any Resistance group. He witnessed the interrogation of a Gestapo informer, and the interrogator turned on him and hit him with the butt of a PPSz and blood spurted from his mouth and nose. After a week of interrogation, they let Stan go. Nobody was safe. A knock on the door in the middle of the night and arrested on any pretext, and nobody knows where you have been taken.

One Friday, Russian officers came to Pac, the blacksmith, so that he could shoe their horse. They were in a hurry, but the fire had died down. He had a 5 litre can of petrol that he splashed onto the fire. The can caught fire and blew the bottom off the can, splashing burning petrol all over his abdomen. He rolled around in the snow and, eventually, they managed to douse the flames. He died the following Sunday. Josef Pac was not only a blacksmith; he would act as a dentist, charging 2 zloty to take aching teeth out.

A mother with four beautiful daughters moved into his house. They had sweet melodious voices. My pal, Henryk Kubit, and I used to visit them occasionally. One of their friends was a young lady from Dukla. Coming up was a big dance night in Dukla. Henryk and I were invited. Meanwhile, Henryk's pal was getting married in the village of Turaszowka, so we went there on pushbikes. It was so crowded there that we left and rode to Szcezepancowa where there was a dance, tanked up on homemade vodka.

On the way we met '*Pimpus*', one of our Resistance members. He had a 1 litre bottle of 96 per cent proof spirit in his briefcase. We drank that between the three of us before going to the dance. When we arrived, it had just started and only one couple were dancing. I danced with a nice little girl we used to call *Kaczka* (Duck) when she was working in Deutsche Luft Hansa. I can't remember much, but suddenly there was a fight, which brought me to my senses. I pulled my pistol out and shot at the ceiling three times.

The fight stopped. A voice shouted, 'Who was shooting?'

I said, 'I was shooting.'

Someone shouted, 'Who are you?'

I said, 'I am *Milicja*', then another voice said, 'Who is *Milicja*? I am the *Milicja*.'

Someone grabbed my fingers, bending them backwards and as I reeled back, somebody pulled the pistol from behind my belt. One of the neighbours, Majchrowski, a strong fellow, was holding the crowd back while Henryk pushed the Russian soldier who was guarding the doors so forcibly that he landed on the floor. I dived out now, quite sober, and ran towards the bushes by the Jasilka River. I lay there for a good while because I knew they were looking for me.

After it had quietened down, I went to one of our safe houses. When Konrad had heard what had happened, the both of us went to a *Milicja* man that Konrad knew personally from before the war and demanded the return of my pistol. He said that he did not have the pistol. We went to see the *Soltys* (head of the village) and demanded that he take positive action to recover the pistol or there would be reprisals. Konrad gave me an old *Mauser*, it must have been left over from the First World War. An awkward thing, with a big square box for a magazine, a small handle, thin pointed barrel and very uncomfortable behind the belt. It was a 9mm calibre. I had to have some form of defence as I was a marked man.

The NKVD and their puppets, *Milicja Obyywatelska* (citizens' militia), were arresting hundreds of innocent people on any trumped-up charge. It was enough that even if you had an acquaintance, or knew a certain person who was suspected of having political views which were not communist, you would be convicted. Many who had jobs in the town hall and other government departments were arrested, including Niemsta, (Kazimierz Czlowiekowski), probably because he was outspoken.

He was sent to Siberia.

58

Elimination of Traitors and Informers

Word had got around that one of the Partisans from another group was betraying all his Partisan mates to the NKVD, the locations of safe houses and hidden stores of weapons. He was from the village of Zeglce. His mother was bragging that he would shortly receive a medal from Stalin for his services. We heard that he had betrayed around eighty people, who were arrested and taken to Russia. After my meeting with Podkowiak, he suggested that I should try to eliminate him. He said, 'Be very careful as he usually has two Russian guards looking after him.' There was a dance in one of the houses on the hill between the villages of Zrecin and Zeglce. There were only three houses in that neighbourhood. Henryk Kubit came with me to the dance, which was in full swing when we arrived. Sure enough, there were a couple of soldiers in uniform. Henryk asked someone who was the fellow (I cannot remember the name of the man we were after), then he whispered it to me.

We had a custom in our area that you could pay the musicians some money and that dance was yours – you could choose anyone you wanted to dance with you and the rest had to watch. I paid the musicians, then invited five couples including the traitor to my dance. While we were talking, I kept an eye on the Russians. The dance ended at midnight.

Outside, Henryk, Msciciel, Litavor and Jelen were walking in front of us. I was following them while talking to the traitor (I think his name started with O… Olszyc?) heading towards a T-junction. About 100yd behind was the Russian soldier. As we approached the junction, he said, 'See you at the next dance.'

He was going right towards Zeglce, while I was going to turn left towards Zrecin.

As we reached the junction, I pulled my *Mauser* and said, 'You bastard.'

'Ty Z Kurwy Synu!' (Son of a whore.)

'How many people have you betrayed?' Then I pulled the trigger pointing at his head.

Once, twice, the third one was a dud, so I ejected it. He uttered something like '*Stasz…*', then I pulled the trigger, a fourth time, and this time it was successful. I heard the blood bubbling. I knew he was dead. I crossed the road to the fields, walking quickly, and joined the road ahead of my pals and waited for them to catch me up.

Henryk walked up to me and asked me, 'Did you do him?'

I said, 'Yes.'

He said, 'I didn't hear anything.'

As we walked towards Zrecin, we heard the footsteps of someone running. It was the Russian soldier.

Panting, he said, 'Who was shooting?'

I said, 'There were a few men in front of us, perhaps they were shooting.'

He said, 'If you have a weapon throw it away.'

Then he shook hands with my pals, but when he shook hands with me, my *Mauser* fell from behind my belt onto the road and when I grabbed it, he ran like the wind. Now, my movement was really restricted, and I had to move from place to place at night. My Russian TT (*Tokarev*) pistol was returned, but I swapped it and the *Mauser* for a Belgian FN which held fifteen bullets – fourteen in a double stack magazine and one in the barrel. It was a 9mm calibre with a leather case.

Our invitation to the posh dance in Dukla was in the next few days. It's quite a long way so we went on the bicycles. When we got there, the guests were high-ranking Russian officers, *Milicja* commandants and civilian dignitaries.

During the interval there was an auction for a bouquet of flowers, which I bought and presented to the young lady who had invited us. Everybody was applauding. We had quite a few drinks as usual. The time came to go home. We did not feel like going home as it was a long way, and we'd had a lot to drink.

A *Milicja* officer approached us and said, 'Why don't you stay in my place for tonight?'

I wasn't quite sure what to do. We were tired after the long ride to Dukla and the dance, so we agreed to stay, not realizing that the officer was the father of the young lady to whom I had presented the bouquet. I was recently in so many dangerous situations that I was willing to risk anything. We were talking in his house, and I told him it was me who shot the previous Commandant of *Milicja*.

He said, 'I got his job.'

He told us that Foremny was much too strict with his own people and that vodka was the only commodity you could trade with the Russians. 'I'm going easy on vodka makers', he said. The next day he gave me three packets of 9mm ammunition for my FN as some of the old bullets weren't 100 per cent reliable, which later probably saved my life.

We then rode home on the bikes. I stopped in a house on the outskirts of Wrocanka village, one of our safe places with '*Mama*', a very pleasant young woman of enormous size. Konrad and Stas were there. Stas and a few of our boys were giving a beating to some arrogant communist Russian servants. One of them was bullying the people, so he had a good lesson and Stas took his Communist Party membership card from him.

He said to me, 'Take it.'

I said, 'What do I want it for?'

He said, 'You never know.'

He insisted that I take it. Shortly after that, Stas got caught and was executed. I could not stay in one place for more than two or three days in case someone saw me, and reported my whereabouts to the NKVD or *Milicja*.

59

Face to Face with the Enemy

Most of the unpleasant events happened to me on Fridays. This one was no exception. It was either 13 or 14 June. I slept in the village of Szczepancowa for two nights, and at around 11am the next morning I was on the move again. It was a drizzly morning with puddles of water and mud on the field track, so I pinned the corners of my gabardine mac with safety pins to the pockets not realizing that my PPSz was showing.

It was a little uphill, so I got off the bike and pushed it until I reached level ground. Suddenly from behind the corn came a loud voice.

'*Tovarish podazhdeey.*' (Wait friend.)

For a moment I froze. I stopped, holding my bike close to my body trying to hide my pistol. He said in Russian, 'Where are you going?'

I said, pointing, 'To that village.'

He said, 'Where did you come from?'

I said, pointing, 'From that village.'

He then said, 'Do you know where we can get a watch mended?'

I said, 'No.'

The lieutenant must have been over 6ft tall and well built.

'You have a weapon?'

I said, 'Yes.'

He said, 'Do you have a permit for it?'

I said, 'Yes,' and showed him the Communist Party membership card, which had an official stamp on it.

He said, 'I can't read that, give me the weapon and I will take you with me.'

A quick decision was necessary. I thought if I wound the two of them, I have a chance. If they take me, I've had it. I rested the bike against me, then carefully pulled the sleeve of my coat so that the automatic was free, hoping he wouldn't notice the pistol. The other Russian who had the rank of staff sergeant (*Starshina*), snatched the automatic then the lieutenant said, 'Give me the gun.'

The pistol was fully loaded and cocked. I took it slowly from the case and, like lightning, shot the lieutenant who was 4ft away. He copped it in his right eye. His hand went automatically towards it. His brain was splattered all over his cape. I immediately turned my gun on the staff sergeant, who tried to shield himself with his hand. He copped three bullets in the face. I immediately grabbed the lieutenant's PPSz and finished off the sergeant. His mouth was open, and he was still breathing.

It was mid-morning, and I was on the outskirts of the village. People came to see what was happening. I waved my hand gesticulating for them to go away. Some of them did while others were still looking on. I pointed the gun at them, and they went.

A minute later, a young lad about 15 years of age and '*Old Nitka*', who was known for his cruelty to horses, turned up. Every horse that Nitka had was reduced to a skeleton within a few weeks. After he was paid for a job, he would stop outside the restaurant drinking, put newspaper into the horse feeder and said to the horse, 'Read that you bastard, the oats are too dear.'

I told the two of them, 'Come here.'

The young lad came over straight away, but Nikta said, 'Mister, I haven't had my breakfast yet.'

I ordered them to come here and drag the bodies into the corn and off the track. After they did that, I took both soldiers' documents and the sergeant's rifle, also a pair of boots. There was a shortage of footwear. I put the lieutenant's cap on my head and started walking to Wrocanka, where Konrad was staying in Mama's house. His wife and daughter came to visit him. As I was on my way, the wife of the Director of the Water Works was passing and asked me in Russian if she could go past. I said in Polish she could go, but not a word to anyone. I proceeded to one of the two isolated houses to wash my face as it was sprinkled with blood. The girl that was there, Helena Zajdel, knew me. I washed my face, then walked to Mama's place. I dropped the weapons in the corn on the way.

I said to Konrad (Janek), 'Quick, get the hell out of here, shortly it will be swarming with Russians, I just shot two of them.'

Quickly, we crossed the Jasiolka River, went into the forest to Orezechowka and stayed there until the excitement had died down. Konrad went first to Bobrka to find out what the situation was there. The news was not good. New arrests, beatings and people disappearing was on the increase. Orezechowka was under suspicion again, so I had to move out. I received a message that I should bring one of the boys to the Krosno area as he was in danger. I was provided with a *Milicjant* uniform and escorted the man as a prisoner. We moved at dusk, then slept in the corn on bare ground. I was as stiff as a board that morning. I took him to Mama's place. He didn't have a weapon with him. Later, I went to Bobrka to see Konrad. There was a letter from my mother; after reading it, I put it in my briefcase which was strapped on the bike. I also had a bar of soap for my mother, it was very hard to get hold of. I hadn't seen my mother for quite a long time, so I went on the bike to see her. I was wearing the *Milicja* uniform so people would not recognize me.

60

Shoot Out with the *Milicja*

As I was riding on the footpath through the fields, I came to a clearing. On my right, at around 50yd, seven *Milicja* men were coming in my direction. I jumped off the bike and turned my automatic on them. Fortunately for them, it was set on single shots. Had it been on serial, most of them would probably be dead or injured. After the first shot they dropped to the ground and several rounds just passed my temple. I could feel the heat as it could not have been more than half an inch from my head. I dived through the corn which was about 5ft high. The plots were 20–30ft wide. I ran across two of them and laid down staying quiet and listening to find out where the shots were coming from. I fired a short burst from my PPSz then ran a little further.

Somehow, I caught the automatic on the corn and it came open. To shoot again, I had to hold it shut with my left hand and pull the trigger with the index finger of my right hand. I couldn't aim properly but still sent a few rounds in the direction of the gunfire, then retreated a little bit further. I headed towards some trees, crossed a stream and climbed up the bank on the other side. Under cover of the corn, I made my way to Mama's place to pick up the unarmed fellow.

Meanwhile, the *Milicja* were spread out all over the place looking for me. Eventually, they must have been shooting at each other because I was a long way from the shootout. They were still shooting when I reached Mama's place. They must have been more scared than me. I can't imagine seven armed *Milijca* going for a walk; they must have been looking for me. Unfortunately, I had to ditch my bike, and the briefcase attached to it, in which was the letter from my mother.

61

My Mother Is Arrested

The *Milijca* went to my cousin's house, where his father was repairing the thatched roof. They ordered him to come down from the roof at once, pushed him about and asked a lot of questions. That evening they came and arrested my mother. They took our cow to a neighbour to look after, threw the cat out, locked the house and put a seal on it. They took my mother to the District Capital, which was Rzeszow, and locked her in the cellars with water dripping through the stone ceiling and lots of rats. They gave her bread and water twice daily, but thankfully they did not beat or torture her. They kept my lovely mother in the cellars for six months. My mother was very religious and took a wooden cross with her, which kept her spirits up. She resigned herself to God's will.*

News reached me that my uncle Antoni (pseudonym '*Kuna*'), who was the editor of the underground press, *OSA*, was arrested, and beaten black and blue, nearly losing his senses. I can imagine what they would have done to me had they caught me.

Our cat, which they threw out, wandered off. Some days later, it approached my pal's mother (who walked in a similar way to my mother) and jumped onto her shoulder, purring. But when it realized that it wasn't my mother, it scratched and bit her face.

---

* At the time of writing, Stan still had the cross. I don't know what happened to it. (Len Czekaj)

62

My Promotion

I was contacted by Podkowiak, who was in close association with the leadership, who promoted me to *Porucznik* (lieutenant) and I was now in charge of OP-11 in the Krosno area.

Konrad hadn't been in touch with headquarters for a long time and was always drunk. They couldn't rely on him. There weren't many Partisans left. Some had given up the struggle whilst others were scattered in various safe houses and were moving from place to place, which made contact impossible. We made two more raids, both to punish German collaborators. The *Soltys* (village leader) from Kroscienko gave us information that someone called Wyzne was very friendly towards the Germans and wanted him punished.

Five of us went in the evening and I told them all to just lay him down on the floor and to take his money and clothes. We did not beat him. The other collaborator lived in the village of Iskrzynia which was a fair distance away. I was told to execute this man as he was a bad one.

The seven of us arrived when the family were having supper and I pointed my pistol at him and said, 'Hold your spoon up to your mouth.'

I was going to shoot him, but when his two young daughters clung on to him and started crying, I didn't have the heart to do it. They were about 12 and 14 years of age. We took some money and valuables from him. I did not like this as it was more like robbery.

It was a nerve-wracking time for most of us. Sometimes, I stayed with Mr and Mrs Sep with whose son, Wladek, I had worked at Deutsche Luft Hansa and who belonged to another Resistance platoon. I slept in their loft on straw and then made my way to Kozielec (Leki Dukielskie) for a few days.

I met up with Henryk Pasterkiewicz (pseudonym '*Maszynista*' or machinist), who said, 'Let's go to a fortune teller, they say she is good.'

I told him I wasn't fussy but went anyway. She took out a large deck of cards, some with strange pictures on them.* She told me my age, I was an only son, and that I was in danger, but will survive, and within six weeks will be out of the country. I thought, I hope this is true but it must be impossible. I could not visualize how this could come about.

---

* Probably tarot cards. (Len Czekaj)

63

Dead or Alive

A message came from Podkowiak that twenty-five plain clothes and uniformed *Milicja* had been assigned to get me 'dead or alive', the reward on my head was 25,000 zloty, and that I should contact Podkowiak at a certain address urgently.

I went as instructed. Podkowiak had some very important news for me.

He said, 'You must move from this area for a while as it much too dangerous for you now. I have arranged a false name, age and birthplace. Your name is now Stanislaw Wozniak, born in Bobrka on 10 August 1919 to avoid conscription. I have also found you some accommodation with the family of Captain Persowski in the village of Odrzykon.'

He was one of the top officials in the town hall there and had supplied the false documents. I went back with the Sep family. I had my Russian TT pistol, a Colt six shooter, plenty of ammunition and two hand grenades.

64

A Dangerous Journey into the Unknown

That late afternoon I kissed Stasia goodbye, shook hands with the others and went cautiously through the fields. I hadn't gone more than 500yd when I saw two heads bobbing up and down, running a couple of fields away. I sat down quietly with my pistol ready and kept silent for about 20 minutes. I was scared now. I had left the two grenades behind as they were awkward to carry, only wearing my suit and no baggage. I could hide the pistols behind my belt but not the grenades; they were too bulky. I arrived in Odrzykon late at night.

The captain and his family were waiting for me. They had made a bed in the loft, and after climbing up, I pulled the ladder up with me. The captain and his wife had two daughters and two sons. The older daughter's name was Genowefa (I think), the younger one Krystyna (I called her Krzysia). The older son was Tadeusz (Tadek) and the young one Bronislaw (Bronek). I was staying in the backroom during the day where Krzysia kept me company, playing with my hair and ears. She put her hand up my trouser leg tickling. I felt very embarrassed. I only came here for sanctuary.

Mrs Persowski was a high school teacher by profession. She had a fine opera singing voice. One day she said, 'I am going to dye your hair, so people won't recognize you.'

She dyed it black.

I ventured to an outdoor dance with Krzysia, which was on the outskirts of the next village. I had plenty of money and we could buy vodka, so we had a few drinks. We had sex under a tree not far from the dance. When we were walking back to the house, we got within 100yd of the door, and she would go no further. I begged her and pleaded with her but to no avail. Her brother came looking for her and hit her, but still, she would not go home. Eventually, her mother persuaded her. I was feeling extremely embarrassed and guilty. I went up into the loft and was ashamed to come down and look them in the eyes.

A company of 260 Russian soldiers moved into Odrzykon so I had to be extra vigilant. I was asked to grind some sweetcorn in a *Zarna* (a hand-operated grinder) which was in the garden shed about 40ft away from the house. Krzysia came to help me, and we grabbed another love session. We had to be careful as the grinding machine made a rumbling sound. Just after we had finished our loving, Tadek came to check on us.

Time was approaching for my migration to the West. I went for a nice walk with Kryzsia for the last time.

65

Migration to the West

The new Polish border, the Oder-Neisse Line, in the west was established. The land vacated by the evicted Germans had to be occupied by someone. So, many who had been evicted from eastern Poland, which had been annexed by Stalin, were resettled there. Many people from other parts of Poland volunteered to move there, including the Persowski family, who were allocated a castle and 200 hectares of land. I was allocated a farm with 40 hectares but, of course, I had no intention of occupying any farm. My aim was to get away from the Krosno area and, if possible, abroad.

After saying goodbye to Mrs Persowski, Gienka and Krzsysia, Mr Persowski and his two sons boarded a hired horsedrawn wagon with me and went to the railway station at Krosno. I was still alert in case someone recognized me at the station, but no one did, and we were on our way. Mrs Persowski and her two daughters were to follow when the others had settled down.

I had my pistol ready and within easy reach under my jacket, behind my belt. Finally, the train set off. It stopped in Tarnow, where the NKVD made random checks, staring in our eyes, but it went without a hitch. They took one person off the train. Our next stop was Krakow. I thought that we were never going to leave. We were there for three days. Three or four times, the locomotive was coupled to more wagons and ready to go, then Russian soldiers would come and take them. After three days in Krakow, we finally arrived in Katowice.

66

That's Where We Parted

I said farewell to Mr Persowski and his sons, thanking him for everything he had done for me. As a token of my appreciation, I gave him my Omega pocket watch. We waved and went our separate ways, never to see each other again.

67

All on My Own

Now I was on my own in a strange town, although I knew Erick Holeczek (*Olejek*) was living here in Katowice. I had his address in my head, so I went to find his place. I could not keep addresses or notes on paper in case of arrest. He had married my cousin Zosia, and they had moved to Katowice with their little daughter, Roza.

I wasn't very welcome in case the NKVD or the *Milicja* traced me to his place. He agreed that I could stay for a few days, providing I did not show my face outside. He found me lodgings with an elderly lady whose husband was lost on the Russian Front. She showed me her furniture, which was damaged by Russian soldiers banging their pistols on the piano and table. She was a nice person though, although they were all nice after they had lost the war.

Many Silesians were *Volksdeutscher* (second-class Germans). When some of them were asked if they were Poles or Germans, they said, 'We don't know yet, we don't know who is going to take over.'

I went for a ride on the tram, then sat on a park bench near the main road. I saw a lovely little puppy running across the road towards me. Before it made it across, a heavy army lorry ran over it. That has stuck in my mind.

68

America Detonates the First Atom Bomb

I went to buy a newspaper and noticed the headlines taking up a third of the front page:

'Atom.'

I can't remember the date, but it was the first atomic device the Americans had detonated in a tower in the desert. I paid a visit to a hairdresser for a haircut and while he was cutting my hair, he said, 'You have had your hair dyed.'

I said, 'Yes.'

As soon as he had finished, I paid him and got away from that area quickly, in case he reported to the *Milicja* that a young fellow had his hair dyed. They would become suspicious and would check who I was. As I wandered around, I noticed a queue of roughly twenty people. I joined the queue and asked them what were they queuing for? I was told passes were being issued for travel to East Germany.

When I came to the window, the man issuing the passes asked me where I wanted to go and why. I told him that my mother was in Berlin, she was not well, so I want to bring her back. He asked me where I had come from. I told him Krosno.

He said, 'I am from Krosno. Come back tomorrow and we can have a chat.'

I went the next day, still suspicious, as I had to be. He introduced himself as an Engineer, Mercik. He came to Katowice before the war. He gave me a pass, dated and stamped. I told him I wanted to get to the West. He said that people do get through and he said, 'Break a leg', which meant 'good luck'.

I went back to my lodgings and, a couple of days later, I found a job working in a garage, telling the owner that I had worked on aircraft engines at Deutsche Luft Hansa. One day after work, I went to a shop about half a mile away to buy some cigarettes. I approached the counter and asked for a twenty pack. Suddenly, and without any warning, I was whacked across the face with great force and a voice shouted, '*Nie uznal ty menia?*' (Why didn't you greet me?)

It was a Russian soldier. A thought flashed through my mind: should I? I had a pistol, which I always carried with me, and in a split second, I could have shot him, but that would have been the end of me. There were hundreds of them everywhere and no way of escape.

I said, '*Zdrastwujtie tovarish,*' (hello comrade) and went out of the shop. It was a close shave. My hate for them grew even stronger now. I went back shaking with hate. I did not regret shooting those two Russians.

Chatting to the men at work, I discovered that Sundays on a disused railway embankment, people were buying, selling and exchanging various items. I went there the next Sunday and found out it was true. People were buying and selling and negotiating prices. There were a few dozen taking part. I sold my pistols and my silver Omega pocket watch (I had given the chrome one to Mr Persowski). I had 6,000 zloty and used some of the money to buy some food.

I acquainted myself with three men and a woman that I overheard talking about working on a farm in Germany, and it was of great interest to me. I discovered that they had the same idea as me, but for different reasons. If I remember correctly, the eldest man's name was Bronek, the other one, Jozek, and the youngest, Wladek. The girl's name was Zoska. She was following Jozek and had a shop in Krakow, which she had left for her mother to look after. Jozek wasn't interested in her band, at the first opportunity, we lost her.

69

Crossing into Czechoslovakia

We fixed a time and date to meet and caught the train to Racibotz near the Czech border. We split up into two pairs so as not to arouse suspicion, meeting back up a bit later at the edge of the town. We walked through fields and woods until late afternoon and came to the small town of Krnov. As we walked up the main street, we were stopped by a Czech policeman who asked us what we were doing there. We said that we were coming home from Germany and had lost our transport.

'That's alright,' he said, 'you are only 20km from the Polish border.'

A Russian NKVD major turned up and asked the police officer in a harsh tone of voice, 'Who are these people?'

The officer told him, and he seemed satisfied with the explanation. He turned to us and said, 'Wait a few minutes and one of our lorries will take you there.'

Within a few minutes, a lorry arrived and took us to the Polish border guard, near Glubczyce. The officer in charge of the border post asked us a few questions and my companions told him about Germany and why they were coming back.

'You must be fools, I wish I could get there,' he said.

70

Back in Poland

They gave us food and chicory coffee, then ordered one of the soldiers to take us to a large block of flats for the night and told us he would see us the next day. We were very tired. He put us in with a German woman whose husband and son were prisoners of war in France.

The next morning, the officer in charge said, 'Anything you want from the Germans, just demand it and if they refuse, just take it.'

The next night, Jozek came into my bedroom and asked me if I would like a woman. I said that I wouldn't mind and then he showed me her bedroom. I went in and she was ready for bed. I really enjoyed it, although I wasn't quite 21, and she was 45 years of age. She must have enjoyed it as well, because the next night she slept with me and not Jozek, all night.

Trying to find the best way out of this situation of being back in Poland, I took a pushbike from a German. The nearest railway station was Prudnik, not very far away. I left the pushbike at the station for safekeeping and returned to our lodgings. We discussed which direction to try next. News was that through the Czech border was still the easiest route, but I reasoned that if we were caught again, we would have no alibi at all, and so I decided against it. My companions were going to try to get through via the Czech border again.

71

We Parted Company

I went to the railway station to get a ticket to Jelenia Gora (southwest Poland). There was a uniformed NKVD man there who asked me if it was my pushbike. I said no. The employee on the station must have told him it was mine. I was glad when the train arrived. The train arrived at Jelenia Gora very late that afternoon. Most of the people must have lived locally, as there were just a few of us left on the platform. A middle-aged man asked us, including a nice Jewish girl, if we had anywhere to stay.

We said no.

'You can stay in the school,' he said.

He must have been either the school caretaker or a teacher. There were six of us and the pretty Jewish girl, so we settled down dozing on the school benches. At least we were inside, out of sight. We were out early the next morning. I had a little piece of bread to eat.

The train to Gierlice (Gorlitz) on the East German border was the one I was waiting to catch. The locomotive was attached to the wagons but not departing yet. I sat on the floor looking at a map.

A Russian army major came and snatched the map from me and said, 'You are a spy.'

I was very frightened because the Russians could pin anything on you and shoot you. Once they have got you, it's almost impossible to get away. He did not take me, but I was like a cat on hot bricks, wishing for the train to depart. It was not to be. Two Russian soldiers came and took the locomotive away. I must have been waiting for four hours before we moved off (to my relief).

72

Crossing into East Germany

When we arrived at Gierlice, all who were going to Germany had to disembark as the train was going farther north. I got off and followed the people across the bombed bridge over the Nisa (Neise). The middle of the bridge was almost touching the water, but there were no gaps, so we crossed it, if a little apprehensively just in case it collapsed. When I got to the German side, I changed my Polish zloty into Deutsche marks at a rate of five to one in my favour. I left myself with 500 zloty just in case something went wrong, and I found myself back in Poland again.

A goods train was waiting on the other side of the bridge, so all of us got in and we were on our way to Dresden. There were crowds of people in the wagons. Two women started a conversation with me. One of them must have been extremely desperate, as she started playing with my private parts, while the other one was shielding her from the gaze of the other passengers. I didn't mind, and it gave her a thrill. Her name was Gerta, or Gertrud, and she gave me her address, which was Dresden Radeboul 2, asking me to visit her. When we arrived at Dresden station, she kissed me and bit my lip, which bled a quite a lot.

I was amazed at the amount of damage caused by the bombing. There were huge steel girders which were part of a dome, twisted like bits of tin with concrete blocks the size of a small room still attached. We came to a huge hall, which was still intact, and sat on the concrete floor. There were hundreds of people. I put my head on my knees, always alert to what was going on around me.

A policeman shouted, 'Always be alert, there are many foreigners and spies about, and you must report anything suspicious to the Police.'

The police then ordered us all to take our papers and documents to the office until morning.

I thought, this is it. They are bound to get me now.

I had no option. We all filed into a large building and slept on the floor in rooms reminiscent of soldiers' quarters or offices. The next morning, fearing the worst, I went with the others to collect my documents, but thankfully there was no problem, as they gave them back without questions being asked.

73

Food Problem

I was getting hungry, so went to the bakers. There was a lovely smell of freshly-baked bread and cobs. Outside the shop on a notice board in five languages, 'No food without a ration book'. I went in and the woman serving asked me if I had the ration book. I said no, and asked if her if she could spare me a couple of cobs, but she wouldn't give me anything. I was desperate now. I went to the butcher's shop and asked if I could buy some *Blut Wurst* (black pudding). I was holding a 100 Deutsche mark note in my hand. He wrapped quite a big parcel under the counter and gave it to me with some change, which I told him to keep as I was just glad to have something to eat. I sat on a park bench and had a good feed.

I met another Pole with the same intentions as me, and we travelled together. I had my rucksack with my gabardine mac and other bits and pieces in it. These were all my possessions, except for my wallet which contained money and documents. I said that he could put his stuff in the rucksack, and we can take turns to carry it.

We travelled by train to Chemnitz and, on the way, I noticed a tall viaduct with half of it missing. When we arrived, we followed a crowd of people walking to the outskirts of the town which was quite a distance. The road was like a largish country road. As we got closer to some buildings, two Russian soldiers armed with automatic weapons were checking documents. I was scared and trying to think of an alibi, but after checking a group of three people in front of us, they went, probably off duty.

My guardian angel was with me…again.

We arrived at a very large building, and I heard someone say that it was a *Schutzstaffel* or SS *Kaserne* (barracks). We were directed to different rooms where there were straw mattresses on the floor, and I had a reasonable sleep after the long walk. We all went out in the morning and the weather was good. I waited for my mate, but there was no sign of him. He had my rucksack and the rest of my belongings.

My next move was to Leipzig which was the next train. I could no longer wait for him. In Leipzig, there was a very large transit camp with a Polish eagle on the front of the building above the entrance, and a Polish guard on the door wearing red and white armbands. I thought, this is a bit of alright, I can have a few days' rest and some food.

Unfortunately, they would not accept strangers, not even for one night. I was disappointed, tired and frightened, not knowing what to do next. In conversation, I discovered that the easiest way to get through to the West was from Eisenach, so my next train to board had to be heading there. When I arrived at the station, there was a train standing in the sidings, full of men returning to their various own countries after they had been freed by the Americans.

They started throwing packets of cigarettes, tins of powdered milk, tins of coffee and other items out of the windows. I caught a tin of coffee. Although I couldn't eat coffee, I put it in my pocket. I was getting hungry now and all I had was money and a tin of coffee but I couldn't buy food. I could not eat. Staying on the station wasn't an option, so I asked around as to where would be the easiest place to cross the border. My excuse was that my mother was in the West and I was trying to bring her back as she was ill. I was told that it was much easier to cross at the British zone, which was further north, as the Russians had tightened up the closer borders.

To get further north, I had to go back to Erfurt, as there were no trains to the north from Eisenach. When I arrived at Erfurt, I sat on a wall by the station. A train arrived with many Russian soldiers and women in uniforms. I saw that they were eating sandwiches, and I asked one of the women if she would give me a piece of bread, but she shouted at me and threatened to report me to the police. I did not wait, and I went wandering about and found a *Gasthaus* restaurant not far away. I was glad to sit in peace. It wasn't long before a nice young lady sat at my table smoking a cigarette. She offered me one, which I readily accepted as I was gasping for a smoke; although I didn't smoke much, my nerves were strained.

I would like to go back to the journey from Chemnitz to Leipzig where I developed a terrible toothache. A German man watching me holding my jaw said, 'I will get rid of your toothache.'

He screwed up a piece of paper, lit it, then blew it out and said, 'Take a good sniff.'

I did and the toothache stopped immediately. I thanked him very much.

Back to Erfurt – I gave her the tin of coffee. She was delighted with it and gave me the rest of the cigarettes she had in the packet. I asked her if she knew of any place I could stay for the night. She told me that there was a guesthouse near the airfield, but it was usually full.

I said, '*Auf wiedersehen*', and went as she had directed.

I found the place and went in, ordered a cup of *ersatz* (substitute) coffee and asked if there were any vacancies.

The man (he must have been the proprietor) said, 'Sorry, all full.'

I took my time drinking the coffee, as it was safer in there than outside. What I heard him saying to the other man working there sent shivers down my spine. Apparently, for the last five nights, the NKVD had woken up every guest checking their documents. Perhaps it was just as well there were no vacancies. I was still taking my time drinking the coffee when a lady came down and hung a key on the board by the door.

The proprietor said, 'You are lucky, there is now one vacancy.'

I was so tired; I had to sleep somewhere and outside wasn't safe. I went straight to my room. But I thought, if they check on me, that's my lot. I had a good sleep, and I was thankful to God and my guardian angel there was no raid that night. I was dirty and hadn't had a decent wash for a long time as I had been travelling constantly.

I didn't want to get involved in conversation with the Germans in case they got suspicious and reported me. I spoke German reasonably well, but they could detect my eastern accent. I told anyone who asked that I was from Katowitz, (Katowice). I went back to the station and, to my amazement, I saw a Polish soldier in uniform. Immediately, I had a suspicion that he was tracking me. I asked him what he was doing here. He said that he had someone in Braushweig (Brunswick) in the British Zone. I told him that I also wanted to go to the West.

We took the train to the town of Halberstadt and from there we took the train to a small place near the border, Dedeleben. It was morning and we were starving. We went to a nearby house and asked if we could buy some food. The lady of the house said, '*Setzen sie sich.*' (Sit down.)

She must have taken pity on us, seeing us worn out and starving. She fried some eggs. It was wonderful. We told her that we wanted to go to the British Zone, and she told us that people do go back and forth. We were shown the direction of the border. It wasn't far.

Caught by the Border

We walked to within 300yd of the border and hid in some bushes, watching the border guards walking back and forth. There were some buildings right on the border to the right of our position. Suddenly, footsteps startled us, and a young soldier looking for a quiet spot saw us.

The soldier said, 'What are you doing here? It's no good lying 300yd from the border.'

I told him that we wanted to go to the British Zone.

'You have to get permission from the War Commandant,' he said.

I asked him where he was, and he told me that he was in the town. We started walking back and then I said, 'Let's walk straight to those buildings and see if they let us through.'

Desperation.

We had walked about halfway towards the buildings on the main road, when two officers on pushbikes riding from that direction stopped and asked us where we were going.

I said, 'To the British Zone.'

His advice was the same as that of the young soldier: Get permission from the War Commandant. We decided to walk back to the station.

The man at the station said, 'Thirty people at a time were going through on a hand track, and two of you can't get through?'

Again, he told us which direction to take and said, 'When you get through the water, you will be in the British Zone.'

Caught for the Last Time

We waited until dark, then we moved quietly through the fields in the direction he had indicated. He had told us to be careful because the border is not straight and even, and people had walked through thinking that they were over it, only to find themselves back on this side. We walked a good distance, when suddenly we could hear footsteps and a voice, '*Pastoy*'. (Stop.)

A shiver went down my spine. Caught again and so near the border. A Russian soldier asked us the same question, 'Where are you going?'

It was obvious, so the answer was the same. 'The British Zone.'

The Happiest Day of My Life

The soldier then said, 'Have you any watches?' We said no. 'Have you vodka?' We told him no.

I said, 'I have money.'

He said, 'I don't want money.'

I thought, that's our lot now. Someone whistled to alert him but, before he ran off, he said, 'Don't go straight on, there is an inspection officer there. Go around, and when you cross two trenches, you will be in the British Zone.' Then he ran off.

We went the way he told us to go, and we ended up in a field of mangles. As we walked through it, they were brushing against our boots and trousers making a rasping noise which started to unnerve us. At last, we came to the trench. It didn't look deep, so I pulled my trouser legs up as high as I could and walked in. It was deeper than I thought, and the water reached my chest. Getting wet didn't matter after that. I kept on going. The next trench wasn't far, and we walked straight in. There was, however, a third trench and then a grassy field.

I said, 'Let's walk as far as we can away from the border, to be sure we are on the right side of it.'

We walked until the lights shining from the border buildings were well behind us. There was a stack of oats in a heap soaking wet, so we hid in that. It may not have been dry, but at least it was warm. It didn't matter at that stage. In the morning, we walked away from the border towards some signs, about 200yd. They weren't in German; they weren't in Russian. They must be English.

At Last, I Am Free

My dream had come true.

We really were in the British Zone, safe from certain death if caught; no more hiding and trying to think up alibis. I thought then, the only way I would come back would be with a weapon in my hand, fighting for a free Poland.

We walked to a small town nearby, asking, 'are we really in the British Zone?' After the answer was 'yes', we went to a baker's shop and bought some cobs. No ration books required. I remember a green lorry pulled up. It was on its way to Braunschweig. The driver said that he would give us a lift, as there was a DP camp (displaced persons camp) there. It was a huge building. It must have been used by the German army or the SS as barracks.

We reported to the camp commandant who asked us many questions. When I told him what was happening in Poland, he got nasty and warned me not to spread 'malicious propaganda'.

He frightened me. I wasn't sure if he could send me back, so I said no more for the time being. At last, I had a bed to sleep in and a decent meal, but I was still afraid in case the camp commandant sent me back. Many from the camp were returning to Poland after forced labour on German farms and in factories.

There were four of us in one room. After a few days, one of them said, 'Let's go to Keine Strasse, there are many prostitutes.'

I agreed and went. I couldn't believe my eyes. I had never seen anything like that before. Women standing in doorways and windows wearing flimsy dresses and waving, 'Kome Rein'. (Come in.)

I saw one dressed in a two-piece suit. She didn't look like a prostitute, but I asked her if she would, and she said, 'Yes.'

Then I asked her, 'How much?'

She said, '30 Deutsche marks, or 50 if I strip off.'

We went upstairs, she stripped off, spat on her fingers, wetting her vagina. This put me right off. I couldn't get an erection although she tried different methods.

She said, 'Come back later or tomorrow', but she wouldn't give me refund.

I didn't bother to go back. When I got back to the DP camp, my mate who went with me to Kleine Strasse said, 'Let's go to the American Zone, they are recruiting Poles for the occupation of Japan, and after two years' service, they will give us American citizenship.'

I had nothing to lose now, so I said OK. We took the train to Frankfurt Am Main for the American army headquarters. At Gottingen, American military police came through the carriage but did not ask for documents. They checked just one or two of the passengers' documents. The train stopped at Kassel where we got off. I had never seen such devastation; there was nothing left, the rubble was 12ft high, and where there was once a street, there was now just a narrow winding path. We found out that there was a DP camp in SS *Kaserne* (the SS barracks).

It was a fair distance from the station on the outskirts of the town at the top of a hill. We told them that we were going to Frankfurt and asked if we could stay for a while. We had a room, and it was a very nice room with clean bedding, much better than the room at the DP camp at Braunschweig.

In the morning, we came down to the dining room where there were long tables covered with white tablecloths. Silver coffee pots, sugar bowls and milk jugs were lined up on the tables. We had cornflakes, bread and butter and coffee. I had never seen anything as posh as this before. Near the exit was quite a large box, half full of strips of condoms in silver paper and they were free. Regretfully, we left the camp after four days on our way to Frankfurt Am Main. We arrived at the gates of the American army headquarters. Two guards in khaki uniforms, white helmets, white gloves, and white garters above their boots. Immaculate. I couldn't understand a word that they were saying.

The only words I knew were 'ok baby'. Somehow, my pal explained our situation to them, and they let us through. As we were walking towards some buildings, two Polish officers were walking toward us. We asked them where the Americans were enlisting Poles for the occupation of Japan. One of them said, 'It's not true, you are wasting your time.' We turned back very disappointed.

The next suggestion my companion made was to go to Freiburg, in the French Zone, and join the Foreign Legion. I had nothing to lose so we went to Freiburg. Again, the military police made random checks of documents but did not check ours. We found the Foreign Legion office upstairs in one of the side streets. Suddenly, I remembered what my cousin Jozek Kubit had told me when he visited my uncle. 'Staszek', he said, 'Whatever you do, never join the French Foreign Legion,' although when he told me that, I never dreamt I would come close to doing just that.

I told my mate what my cousin had told me, and I said, 'I don't think I will go in.'

He went up the stairs and that's the last I ever saw of him.

78

Aimless

I was on my own again, not knowing where to go next. I went back to the railway station and the next train was to Nurnberg. I got on it. It was a bolster train, which usually carried steel or lengths of timber. Quite a few people travelled on it. I lay down in the middle of the wagon to stop me rolling off in case the driver braked suddenly. The train arrived in Nurnberg in the morning, and I found out that there was a large DP camp in SS *Kaserne*.

I jumped on the *strassenbahn* (tram) and reported to the office. I was allocated a room with two others. One was middle-aged and the other was around my age. They gave me some bread and dripping which was delicious. I settled down quite comfortably. They listened to what I had to say about the conditions in Poland and I think that they believed me, unlike the camp commandant at Braunschweig.

Outside the barracks, in a fenced off area, were standing many big and small guns, now redundant. There were about twenty of them. In the camp were hundreds of men and women, some from forced labour and some from concentration camps – many of them intending to stay in Germany and some intending to return to Poland. But the future was so uncertain for all of us. The main thing was that now we were free. I was very happy that I was in no immediate danger of being arrested, tortured or shot, and had my own bed and regular meals.

We had several dances which were enjoyable. One of the men told me that, when the Americans freed them from the concentration camp, they could have three free days to do whatever they want to the Germans without bearing the consequences. He said that they some took revenge on *Bauers* (farmers) who had maltreated them, and some farmers were even killed. One man named Cebula told me that they stole a cow from a farmer, put boots on it and took her to the first floor of a house. The police didn't look for a cow on the first floor. Many of the camp residents went back to Poland to their wives and parents. As for me, I was glad to be here.

One of the men in our section told me that an American labour company needed men. The next day I took a tram (*Strassenbahn*) to Langwasser, where their offices were situated. Through an interpreter I told the manager my name, Stanislaw Wozniak, then he said, 'Start tomorrow.'

On a board outside the offices, in large letters, was: THE 1888 LABOUR COMPANY.

Outside was a fierce looking sergeant with very dark features, perhaps Maltese or Italian, shouting orders to the lorry drivers. There was another chap from the camp starting at the same time. When we got to the site, we were shown our triple bunk beds, set up in a huge hall. We were issued with green overalls and hats.

The next morning, we set off to work just a few minutes' walk away. There must have been 20–30 acres designated for food supplies next to the railway embankment and, from there, a network of steel chutes resting on trestles pointing in various directions. At each end, men, directed by American soldiers, were stacking them and covering them with tarpaulins. The work was easy. The most irritating thing for me was the continuous blaring of jazz music every evening until 10pm.

We were issued with American army meal kits. The lunch was twelve different items of food set out in a row. If there was one I did not like or want, I just passed on to the next one. At the end of the food line were four large churns, each with a ladle hanging from it. They contained orange, grapefruit, pineapple and tomato juices. We could drink as much as we wanted.

Every week or fortnight (I can't quite remember), we had a supply of 200 cigarettes: Raleigh, Chesterfield, Camel, Lucky Strike or Phillip Morris (in brown packets), forty cigars and three packets of moist, sweet-smelling tobacco. They issued us with very smart khaki uniforms and shirts and cream-coloured ties for going out.

Next to our workplace was a camp for Black soldiers. Many of them were lorry drivers. A woman with a shopping bag and three children passed by the Black soldiers' camp. She went into the woods with one of the Black soldiers, leaving the children behind. After a while she came out with her shopping bag bulging. Sex for food?

Many of the boys had German girlfriends who had very little food, so they started to steal various items, mainly sugar, coffee, chocolates and cigarettes. When the Americans realized what was going on, they started searching us on the way out. Anyone caught stealing was put in a cage of barbed wire outdoors, so that everyone could see them. They were there day and night. I don't know how long they were caged or what happened to them after. On the other side of the stores, separated by fields, was a prisoner-of-war camp of Polish ex-prisoners of war, who worked in the warehouse.

They were a crafty bunch; they would tie string to a box of chocolates or cigarettes during the day, pushing the string through the barbed wire fence. Come the evening, they would, from outside the fence, pull on the string and get the goodies. That didn't last long. The Americans got wise to it. Then they found another way, this time on a large scale. They bribed the mainly Black lorry drivers to bring whole lorry loads of assorted goodies into the camp, for which they paid 10,000 occupation marks. After the lorry was unloaded, they drove it out and dumped it.

Once or twice, they were cheated. The back of the lorry was stacked high, but the rest of the lorry was empty, it just looked fully laden. When the next lorry arrived, someone shouted, 'military police'.

The driver legged it and they had the goods for free. One of our men being searched started to run. He was rugby tackled and out fell two 5lb bags of sugar. It was against my principles to get involved in this stealing.

79

Brygada Świętokrzyska

News reached me that the Polish Provisional Brigade (*Brygada Świętokryzyska*) had moved to the forest on the outskirts of Nurnberg. Naturally, at that time, I thought that there would be war with Russia very soon and my aim was to fight my way back to Poland. Immediately, I went and joined them. I oversaw a team in a company of soldiers.

After a few days, I was given an order to get a supply of food and cigarettes for the platoon. Somehow, during transit from the supply tent to the distribution tent, one of the boxes of chocolates and three cartons of cigarettes went missing. I had to report to the *Rotmiszcz Miecz* (cavalry captain) who was in charge. I had tears in my eyes when facing him because I was honest and I trusted people, and this incident upset me. I was told off then transferred to Wujek's tent (Uncle). It was nice and peaceful there. There were only four of us in the tent. My job was to make the daily report along with another officer cadet. (I have his photo dated 15/11/45 Nurnberg.)

Although I was a lieutenant during the Russian occupation, when joining the brigade, I told them that I was an officer cadet rank corporal. I did not want any responsibility after the strenuous last few months full of danger. I wanted it easy for a while. Wujek was a very kind and very religious man, very talented. He used charcoal for drawing religious pictures of angels and Holy Mary, and rays of sun shining through the clouds.

The adjacent tent was occupied by the 1st and 2nd lieutenants. The next tent was used for the orchestra to practice. In charge of the orchestra was A.S. Edward, a lieutenant who played the cornet. (Later, he lost his arm in a motor accident with a Jeep but still managed to play with one hand.) He also had a nice singing voice. Another man, Wenek, was a clarinet player. There was also a famous drummer, whose name escapes me. He could play several other instruments including the guitar, violin and accordion. A very talented musician.

80

My First Romance

A young German girl used to collect our shirts to get them washed, and one day she asked me to take her for a walk. It was my first opportunity for many weeks to have a bit of sex (since the prostitute on the border) which I very much enjoyed. Next time, we did it in her home. However, it became far too serious and when I stopped seeing her, she complained to our chaplain, but that was the end of the romance.

One afternoon, a big lorry fully loaded with 5gal petrol cans caught fire. Some of the exploding cans were hurled high in the air. It was on the edge of a pine forest. Fortunately, it didn't catch fire. There wasn't much to do in Wujek's tent, and I was getting bored. I asked Wujek if he would transfer me to the company. I was put in the sergeants' tent, where I met Sergeant Ignacy, who was from another detachment of Partisans from the Krosno area. He also knew the headmaster, Michajluk who was from Glojsce, where my cousin Anna used to teach. Michajluk was lost in the 1939 campaign, but Ignacy met him in Germany, still alive. At that time, one of the sergeants who was a dispatch rider died, when his motorcycle hit the back of an army lorry.

Every morning after roll call, we sang, '*Kiedy hanne wstaja zorse.*' (In the distance day is breaking.) Exercises next, and then marching and singing. At that time our task was guard duty around the camp. One day after I had finished my shift, I met a girl outside the camp. Her name was Berta, she invited me to her lodgings where I enjoyed the luxury of a nice bed, scoring well. The next afternoon, she came to me crying; her landlady had thrown her out and she had nowhere to go. I had a word with the soldier on guard duty and smuggled her into our tent. The camp beds were close together, so she slept with me. The inspection officer came in and I am sure that he noticed somebody under the blanket, but he just walked out. She was there for ten days when the order came that we were moving to Kitzingen for guard duty.

81

Destination Kitzingen

In the morning, lorries arrived, our kit was loaded, and the convoy was on its way. I don't know why, but we went past Wurtzburg initially. Whether a road or bridge was damaged causing us to detour, I don't know. Wurtzburg was absolutely smashed and only the shells of buildings remained. We arrived at the barracks on a hill, around one and a half miles from the town. It was a nice change to have nice warm quarters instead of tents. I was promoted to Proxy Platoon Commander but still having the rank of Corporal Officer Cadet.

In one of the buildings was an American army detachment. They manned the gate and had overall command. Our duties were to guard a 'vehicle cemetery', where there were many thousands of all kinds of vehicles discarded by the Americans, also some German tanks. Many of these vehicles were in good order and the men used to drive them around. They all wanted to go there on guard duty as they found lots of 'goodies' in the vehicles – cameras, watches, radios and jackets etc., even pistols.

I remember some of the lieutenants' pseudonyms: *Brzoza* and *Jaxa* (Jaksa), a sergeant, *Ptasik*. There was a very fierce regimental sergeant major with a handlebar moustache, but I can't remember his name.

It was night, Ptasik was on guard duty in the cemetery, and I was in the guard house. He reported in every hour. We used to jokingly call each other names. He called me something (it escapes me) and I said, 'Kiss my arse.'

From the other side of the guard house came a thundering voice, 'I've got a son older than you, and you are telling me to kiss your arse? Report to me in the morning.'

It was the regimental sergeant major. However, there was no punishment. He laughed it off.

One morning, I was called to the main gate. I had a visitor. I wondered who it could be. It was Berta. She found out where the company was sent and followed us. I managed to persuade the officer on duty to let her stay. There was a spare room where they kept surplus furniture, beds, chairs and tables and although it wasn't heated, it was better than nothing. One of the corporals asked me if he could sleep with her. I let him try to see if she was willing. She did, although she denied it later. It gave me a good excuse to throw her out. A few days later, she came up to the gate again and wanted to talk to me. She said she now had nice lodgings with a widowed mother and her daughter. She invited me over and asked if I could bring a friend for the daughter. One of the lads who looked the spitting image of Clark Gable came with me, but I did not fancy her anymore. Anyway, there was no opportunity for love making with the landlady around.

We went to get some wine which we exchanged for some American cigarettes. We both had two stripes on our shoulders and the Americans saluted us. They must have thought we were captains. Three of them asked if we knew any *frauleins*. I said I can get one for you if you come with me.

My mate, I and three Americans went to Berta's house, and I said, 'Berta, I've finished with you. You have three to choose from.'

She picked the biggest. My pal was still visiting the landlady's daughter. I went with him on one of his visits to see Berta and I told her what a good turn I'd done for her. She was well looked after, he gave her food, cigarettes and money. It appeared to me that she was pregnant.

One day we had a visit from our colonel in chief. After a speech, all the officers and officer cadets lined up and he kissed every one of us.

Our company moved to Bamberg, where again we had good quarters and not many duties – just as well, as the winter was very hard.

Some news, I found out that there was a DP camp in Bamberg and that my cousin Tadek had left to return to Poland the previous week. It would have all been so much different if I had met him.

I was promoted to Sergeant Officer Cadet, still Proxy Platoon Commander. Each of the sergeants was given a Polish English dictionary and a Learn Book. I developed eczema and was taken to a Polish army hospital on the outskirts of Nurnberg. I was there for three months. It would get better, and then get worse again, and it spread to my hair. I didn't mind. I was learning English and had rations from the hospital and the company.

My English was improving fast. I was learning the correct way. Not just from hearing it spoken. We organized a chess tournament which I won. I won twenty games, and one was drawn against the weakest opponent. We also played cards. In the evening, we would go out looking for frauleins and there were plenty of them. Two of us went by train to visit one of the girls at home 30km away and, this time, the mother did not mind that we made love. We gave them chocolates and cigarettes, which made them happy.

I am sure that the Polish army doctor was experimenting on us. He put me in front of an X-ray machine, switched it on and described to the sergeant, and the sergeant was taking notes. The words I remember were '*bronchitis chronica*'.

One time I brought a young girl to the hospital through a hole in the fence. I got my mates to wake me before the nurses started their rounds. I found three lice on the bed sheets after she went. I was cured at last and returned to the company, but not for long.

82

Girl Trouble

Two of us sergeants had very nice quarters. My room-mate was on duty. One of the privates said, 'I've got two girls, do you want one of them?'

Instead of taking them to my quarters which were never inspected, we took them to the privates' quarters. As we were making love, a captain and an inspection officer who were on duty came in and shone their torches on us.

He said, 'Report to me at 9am tomorrow.'

I reported as ordered and he demoted me to Corporal. A corporal was told to cut off my stripes. He seemed to enjoy it. I was sentenced to four days detention in the cellars. When I came out, I asked the captain to discharge me from the company. He refused. I had no intention of remaining in this company and I asked the secretary to give me some leave forms. He gave me a dozen. They became very useful. I filled one in and signed the captain's name and took a train to Nurnberg with my kit.

I went to the American Stork Club, virtually opposite the railway station, where I had my meals which were excellent, and my sleeping quarters were 500yd up the road. I did this for ten days, but I think they were getting suspicious. I saw an unusual sight; a soldier in a skirt. Everybody was looking at him. A Scotsman. I was talking about the Scotsman to a nice girl who was leaning against the moat wall. She was waiting for the train to Pushendorf which was not due for another two hours, so I suggested we take the *Strassenbahn* (tram) to the *Tier Garten* (zoo). She agreed and later we went for a stroll in the nearby woods and made love.

From then on, I saw her every evening after she had finished work in an office. Her name was Gertrud Kohler. She was a decent young lady, but I didn't think seriously of romance or marriage. Meanwhile, I had many girls during the day. There was nothing else to do. I spent the time in restaurants or in the railway station waiting room. There were still many civilians hanging around who did not want to return to Poland, and a few homeless German youths who gave me information on where to sleep. Several times we slept in a dry cavity in the side of the moat. The young Germans said that it wasn't the Germans who were the war criminals, it was the British and Americans for bombing civilian targets.

One day in a *gasthaus* (guesthouse) in town, I met Frau Kasperek, who was a typist for Deutsche Luft Hansa in Krosno. She used to go out with *Obermeister* Runge. I asked her what had happened to him, and she said that the last time she had seen him was in Berlin.

83

Back in the Polish Guard Company

I joined the 1125 Polish guard company, this time using my real name instead of my false name (Stanislaw Wozniak). I did not mention the past and joined as a private. I couldn't be bothered with leadership. I preferred the careless life. Shortly, our company was transferred to Auerbach, a small town compared to Nurnberg. We took over the duty of guarding 400,000 SS prisoners of war from the Americans. A huge area was surrounded by a double barbed-wire fence with rolls of barbed wire between them. Inside the prison grounds was a white line about 10ft from the fence where no prisoner was allowed to cross, or they would be shot.

There were twenty-four towers armed with machine guns around the outside of the camp. The inside was divided with barbed wire into cages, with a guard by each entrance. In one corner of the camp were 400 SS women prisoners. They would climb onto the flat roof of their quarters and lay naked sunbathing, which made the guards on the towers very frustrated. The guards at the entrance to the cage were also fed up, as they had no peace from the sex-starved women. I was told that the previous company had shot three prisoners who had stepped inside the white line as they did not heed the warning from the guardsmen. The other prisoners tried to pull them back, but when they had a machine gun pointed at them, they retreated.

Our quarters were looked after by SS prisoners. They made our beds, cleaned our shoes and washed our utensils. German SS officers looked after our officers' rooms. A sergeant who had been a *Messerschmidt* fighter pilot was assigned to our room. When the boys used to mess around after he had tidied up, he told us off. He seemed quite friendly, but most of them were after they had lost the war.

When we had time off duty, most of us went to the town about two miles away and we would cadge a lift from the multitude of jeeps and lorries going back and forth. There was an American club in the town open 24 hours, and anyone in an American uniform could have as many ring doughnuts and Coke as they could consume. One day when I was in town, people were staring at a big woman and a young girl, about 13 years old. I asked the woman next to me.

'Who is that?' I said.

'That's Frau Goring and her daughter.' (Hermann Goring's wife and daughter.)

We had quite a lot of time off duty, so one day the boys asked me to go horse riding with them. I said, 'I have never ridden before.'

He said, 'They have quiet horses for novice riders. It's only two Deutsche marks per hour.'

I went and was given a good-natured horse. We crossed a disused artillery range. When the horses started trotting, I was all over the place, holding the horse tight, but when he started galloping, I was OK. After a couple of riding sessions, I quite enjoyed it. A fellow named Wolowik and I went riding in the countryside and met two girls. He had the older one and I had the nice ginger one called Pauline Wind. At first, she was reluctant, but later I got to know her very well. Another one was Erna Hollerer. She was the one I loved a lot, and there were a few others besides. There wasn't much else to do. We did go deer hunting with rifles but when I had one in my sights, I didn't have the heart to shoot it.

Some of us were assigned to deliver 200 SS prisoners to Hof. After the delivery, the American lieutenant in charge treated us to a night in a hotel and a show. He also gave us two days' rations wrapped in brown waxed packets. Before the show, lines of pretty girls were dancing and doing high kicks to the music. I had never seen that before. Although I was quite contented there, I was concerned and in fear of being kidnapped as we were very near the East German border. The boys I remember were Makiela, Szejgis, and Frank Kozera Wolowik.

The air in that area was crisp and fresh, due to the surrounding pine forests. It did not last long; 600 prisoners of war arrived from America to be discharged. Gradually, the Americans replaced our guards with Germans, including the SS guarding their own, which did not make sense to us.

84

Back in Nurnberg

Our company was transferred to Nurnberg Ziegelstein on the edge of the town. We had various duties, from guarding wagons at the railway station, the homes of American families, a hospital for German VIPs and guarding top Nazis in the Nurnberg fortress, the war criminals. Our American commander was James H. Goodsell, First Lieutenant Infantry Commanding 1890 Labour Supply Co. My number was PFC 30963. This was 192 Labour Supervision Centre. I am still in possession of the details of the clothing issued to me and signed off by Lieutenant Goodsell and myself. One of our duties was to guard the guest house rented by the major in charge of supplies for the area. He only used it intermittently and sometimes when he was drunk (according to his housekeeper).

It was very cold walking around outside, so we would stay in the garage. His housekeeper was a lovely lady, Frau Emi Zenger. One morning she came to the garage and asked me if I would like a cup of coffee. I said that I couldn't in case the inspection officer checked up on us.

She said, 'He won't be around yet, I know when he is due so come in.'

We had a nice cup of coffee, cakes and a nice chat. Just before the guard was due to change, she came into the garage and asked me if I would escort her home. She waited for me where we agreed.

Her address was Moss Strasse 13 Ziegelstein. She would not take me into her house, probably because she was ashamed to go out with a soldier. Next day when I was on guard duty, she told me that she was moving into the guest house I was guarding and, when the major was away, I could stay there. I did and it was a beautiful friendship. She was a stage actress and mingled with high society. Her husband was an SS lieutenant lost on the Russian Front. She showed me many photos of her acting on stage.

I was moved to guard a different place, a large house where Russians involved with the Nurnberg Trials were previously staying. That house was haunted. I was inside a room on the ground floor which was paved with quarry tiles. The room was empty, and the door was closed. I could quite clearly hear footsteps and the floorboards creaking. There was no one there. The lights on the very top floor switched on and off, although the place was empty. Once I took a girl into the house and had sex, which was fine, but used a 'pro kit' which we had in our PX store. I was OK, but three of the other boys got VD (the kit's contents were to protect soldiers from venereal disease, and included ointment, cloth, and a cleansing tissue). Three guardsmen were gassed in that house.

A few of us were ordered to Lieutenant Goodsell's house to move some equipment. For the first time I saw a toilet with a fountain in the middle. I guessed what it was for.

85

Stormy Romance

One evening I took the *Strassenbahn* (tram) to town. It was full inside, so I stood on the platform. Near to me just inside was a pretty ginger girl. When I smiled at her, she turned her head towards the window. I put my head outside looking through the window and smiled again. When we got off, we started chatting. Then I grabbed her and kissed her. We made a date for the next day and went for a walk by the river and made love. Her name was Margarete Plank.*

She must have been born out of wedlock as her mother's name was Frau Schwarz. They lived on Obere Kieselberg Strasse 15, 2nd floor Plarer Nurnberg. One day, she suggested that I should visit her at night, and she would sneak me in quietly. I did. I was woken up in the morning by loud shouting. It was her mother. She came into the bedroom and saw me and shouted at Margarete.

I got dressed and said, '*Das tut mir leid*' (I am sorry about that), kissed her hand and went.

I thought that was the end of our romance. Three days later, Marga, as I called her, came to the company's gate asking for me. I came out and she said, 'My mother has invited you to tea.'

I went and 'Mother' was not so bad after all. There was a baby in the cot.

I said, 'Whose baby is that?'

She said, 'Mine. His name is Jurgen and his father is an American soldier, Morris.'

That did not worry me. All I wanted was some company and sex and it was there in that apartment. Her mother was working so, when I had time during the day, the apartment was all ours. One morning she cooked me breakfast using her monthly ration of food. The romance was now solid, and we enjoyed it day after day with no interference.

---

* Stan had 'M.P.' tattooed on his arm, much to my mother's disgust. (Len Czekaj)

86

It's Time to Post Some News Home

I risked writing a letter to my neighbour Dygutowicz in Glowienka, using an assumed name, describing things in a roundabout way so that they could guess it was me. I signed my name as '*Jablonski*'. Professor Jablonski was my maths teacher. It caused enormous joy and anticipation, although they still weren't sure it was me. My mother probably thought that I was dead and the UB (*Urzad Bespieczenstwa*, Polish secret police agency, 1945 to 1954) and the NKVD were still after me.

They often called at my mother's house looking for me. When my mother wrote about it, she said, 'The guests have been visiting again.' She described the many arrests which were being carried out as, 'He/ she was on a tour to see the rising sun for x number of years' – in other words, to Siberia.

They found the concrete pipes under the side of the house, but they were empty. They visited my mother for four years on and off. Most of the letters were censored. Meanwhile, I was enjoying life. During the day when I was off duty, I spent the day with Marga and with Emi at night, when possible, until late one night when the major came in drunk, and I just managed to sneak out the back way. From then on, she wouldn't risk sleeping there anymore and she found bed and breakfast accommodation, but it was cold and uncomfortable.

I was still having an affair with Marga whenever possible, until I felt a burning feeling when passing water as my tube was blocked with a puss-like substance. My mates told me that I had gonorrhoea. It was bad, so I went to the American army hospital, and the test proved positive. I stayed there overnight and was given five penicillin jabs, one every four hours. They gave me a nice dressing gown and I had an excellent breakfast.

After that, I went back to the company. When I saw Marga next, I slapped her face and told her that I didn't wish to see her again.* Then I told Emi that she should see a doctor as she may be infected. It shook her, but we still made love. She did not get infected. At that time, venereal diseases were widespread in Germany with all the different nationalities intermixing. The war had made many widows, and many wives without partners due to their husbands being incarcerated in prisoner-of-war camps. Women needed it badly.

---

* Six years of German and Russian occupation, and Stan's Resistance days, had a brutalizing effect on him, as it did on most people. He was on many occasions existing in a kill-or-be-killed environment. Not knowing if he was going to survive on a daily basis, his behaviour towards women was shaped by this brutal existence, and mirrored the attitudes of men at the time. Thankfully, these attitudes are not tolerated today. As he says in his foreword, he wrote it honestly as it happened, and wanted readers to know what life was like at that time. (Len Czekaj)

87

I Am Afraid Again

I was summoned to appear before the American CIA or FBI, I am not sure which. There were three of them and they asked me many questions. They wanted to know everything. Rumours were going around that they were sending some people back. I was frightened, as that would have been the end. Prolonged torture and execution. Not long after that I was ordered to go to Ingolstadt to be interrogated by Polish officers. I was just getting over the flu and didn't feel well, but I had to go. After the interrogation, I took the train back to Nurnberg.

The train was full and there was a big crowd on the platform. Further down the platform next to the nearest carriage was a beautiful young blonde girl blowing kisses. As there were so many people on the platform, I didn't take much notice, but she kept on, so I pointed to myself, and she nodded. I called her over. She was really beautiful, and offered me a Lucky Strike (cigarette), then gave me the packet. We boarded the train and got off at Nurberg and we took the tram together to Ziegelstein.

There were empty wooden quarters about 50yd from ours where the Americans used to stay, so I took her there. Her name was Karin Hartman. She said she was Czechoslovakian and spoke to me in the Czech language. It's so like Polish that, spoken slowly, a Pole should understand it. I was really in love with her straight away. She was something special.

The next morning, I took some food and she stayed there out of sight. We made love constantly. With most women, it had to be a fairly long break between sessions but with Karin it only took a few minutes. I was so in love with her that I would have done anything she asked, even kill. All the boys were jealous, even the lieutenant who asked me to let him have her and that he could look after her better than I could, which was true – I didn't have the means to look after her properly, but no way would I let her go. I found her lodgings and when I went to her room to make love, the horrible landlady called the police, and they took her away. They could do nothing to me. She used to call me *Starzyku*. She told me that in a few weeks' time, she was going back to Czechoslovakia. Probably just as well, as I wouldn't have lasted much longer having all that sex.

During the war, our cooks were in a prisoner-of-war camp in Germany. Near the end of the war, there was a lot of bombing and strafing by the British and American air forces. One of the trains was bombed and one of the wagons contained German Deutsche mark notes. The cooks filled their suitcases with the money, just in case it would still be legal tender after the occupation. It was. The Americans introduced the 'occupation mark' which they exchanged at the rate of five to one. They bought houses and lived a life of luxury. Most of the people believed that after losing the war, the Deutsche mark would be worthless.

Our meals did not vary much, except Sunday was a little better. Powdered eggs and black coffee with bread and butter was breakfast. Dinners varied slightly.

88

I Was Put in Jail

Our platoon was assigned to guard German VIPs in a hospital. We stayed in a *Kindergarten*, a school opposite the hospital. While we were off duty, a few of us went for a stroll to an adjacent small park. Sitting on a park bench were two American soldiers with two German girls.

One of the Americans shouted, 'Hey Polak, give me a cigarette.'

I said, 'I haven't got one.' (Which was true.)

He said, 'You fucking Polak.'

I went over to him and socked him on the jaw. The fight started and the girls ran for help. There were 2,000 Americans stationed about 100yd away. More of our boys came with rifles, including the lieutenant in charge, and they were hitting out with their rifle butts. One of the Americans hit my left side in the ribs. There must have been twenty of us fighting them.

Sirens wailed, and a dozen Jeeps with military police came from all directions. We were interrogated by the officer in charge, and I answered, as I was the one who could speak English and German the best. As I was talking, I felt my left foot squelching in my boot. It couldn't have been water; there was no rain, and we hadn't walked through any puddles. The soldier who had hit me in the ribs, had stabbed me.

Anyway, I was the one to blame according to the officer in charge, and three of us were taken to Nurnberg jail. They put all of us in one cell. It was horrible being locked up when there was beautiful weather outside. Two nice MPs were on duty, threw cigarettes into our cell while we were asleep; one was black, and the other was white. Later, our boys brought us plenty of cigarettes when they came to visit us. We had sixteen days in jail until the trial, which was in Furth, northwest of Nurnberg.

The American judge who had the rank of colonel said, 'For the attack on an American soldier, I sentence you to six months' – my knees sagged – 'to be served in your company.' Relief.

Makiela and the other Pole were released without punishment. However, it was an experience in jail. We used to lift each other up to the window near the ceiling to watch the other prisoners on exercise and the women peeling potatoes and singing.

Not long after I had served my sentence, I was again in jail, but this time it was to guard the war criminals. There was a fortress inside the jail. A 20ft-high, 5ft-wide wall with steel railings around it and that's where we kept guard. I saw them one morning walking around with many armed American guards watching.

That's the second time that I had seen Hermann Goring, only this time as a prisoner and not as the boss of the Luftwaffe. We kept guard outside around the wall, and the Americans kept guard inside. There was a round hole in each cell door and an around-the-clock guard was kept on each door.

During our break, we played cards with the Americans. One of the guards joined us for a game of poker. We won some and lost some, but just before we were due back on duty, he dealt us very good hands, but the best one for himself. After bragging so much, some of the players stashed, and after his hand was called, his was the best and he won most of the money. He then asked each of us how much we had lost and gave us all our money back. He pulled a big wad of notes from his back pocket and there must have been thousands of occupation marks. He was from Chicago.

One of the platoons was sent to guard some railway wagons on the siding. There was one guard assigned to each wagon, but one of the wagons had four guards. They became curious and opened the wagon and found it contained cases of gold watches which were supplied to officers for $60 per watch. There were 250 watches in each case. The four guards took a case each and vanished. I was told that one of our boys, who was on guard duty at the time, was accused that some goods had gone missing while he was on duty. He took it to heart so much that he put his rifle under his chin and pulled the trigger. He was a very quiet, intelligent fellow.

We had a bully in the platoon, a big strong man with one good eye. He would push some of the boys around, demanding cigarettes and money. Eventually, they snapped and decided to wait for him. As soon as he appeared, they threw a blanket over his head and beat the hell out of him with their army belts. There was no more bullying.

I was called to the gate one day and told that someone wanted to see me urgently. It was Marga. She asked me if I would go with her to the *Gasthaus* to have a talk. I did go and we were friends again. She gave me two watches as a gift, which were from her brother who was a jeweller. I went to her flat one day when her mother was working, and one of her friends whose name was Hilda came to visit her. While Marga was preparing a snack, I was making love to Hilda in Marga's bed. She came back and caught us, and she started hitting me and pulled me off Hilda. Then she wanted me to make love to her. Which I did.

Two of our platoons were moved to the next town, Furth Bay, which wasn't far, more like an extension to Nurnberg as it was connected by the tram. We occupied two large buildings. A lovely town with a park in the horseshoe bend of the river. Marga must have loved me because she found lodgings not far away so that I could spend time with her. She was sex mad and even bribed a woman attendant in a female toilet block so that we could make love. When we travelled on the train, she had her hand in my pocket, the pocket with a hole in it. She went to visit her brother for three days (so she told me), and asked her friend to look after me.

When she returned and the friend told her that we had made love, she went berserk and she said, '*Ich sheise nach diese kameradschaft.*'*

After that, she was more for me than ever. She brought me some scrap gold rings from her brother and took me to a jeweller to get some wedding rings made. The jeweller made the rings while we waited. He measured our fingers, heated the rings up with a small blow torch and stretched them over a cone until they were our size. Marga thought that if I wore a

____

* This roughly translates as 'you have shit on this relationship'. (Len Czekaj)

wedding ring, it would stop me going with other women. Unfortunately, during a break from guard duty, I lost the ring playing pontoon, as well as two watches and 6,000 marks.

It was a disastrous night for me. She was very upset but forgave me.

While I was out walking, I had to answer the call of nature, but I was nowhere near a public toilet. I went onto a building site and found a toilet, where, scrawled on the wall, were these words:

'Unten dem haus wohnt ein geist er jeder der zu lange sheist von unten in die eier beist'

This roughly translates as: 'There is a ghost living in this house who will bite anyone who shits for too long in the balls.'

He didn't bite me in the balls, I shit on his head!

It was an unlucky time for me in Furth. I had a terrible toothache and went to a German dentist. She gave me an injection and asked me to wait 10 minutes. When the ten minutes had elapsed, she tried to prise the tooth out with a spiked instrument. It still hurt, so I had more injections and was asked to wait a further twenty minutes. It still hurt so she decided to give me gas. She put a cloth over my mouth and asked me to count to thirty and when I reached thirty, start again from one. I did manage to count to seven but no more. I was still conscious because I heard and felt the tooth break and fall to the floor. When I told her, she said that I must be very highly strung. Shortly after the tooth episode, I came down with very bad tonsillitis. It was terrible. I had a high temperature, couldn't swallow and the smell from my throat made the boys keep well away from me. A German doctor gave me some tablets and I recovered.

After six weeks in Furth, we returned to another part of Nurnberg. While on duty, Marga came and wanted the usual, so we made love in an empty building nearby. Someone must have reported it because I was told unofficially by one of our corporals.

My next duty was the night shift, and as I was dozing off, I was very tired, the sergeant who was on inspection took the magazine from my rifle. He reported me to our captain, who in turn reported me to his

American boss, First Lieutenant James. H. Goodsell. I was dismissed from the company 'for the good of the service'.

I was able to keep some of the clothing for which I paid (it was deducted) 181.5 marks ($18.50). I deposited my three kit bags at Nurnberg railway station. I had nowhere to stay.

89

Homeless Again

Someone told me that guard companies in Passau on the River Danube were accepting anyone for guard duty. So Marga and I went there. It wasn't true that they accepted everyone. They gave us a meal and suggested we try Munchen (Munich) or go to Austria, but they warned me that Austria were sending people back to their own countries forcibly, so Munich it was. Munich is a big city so we went to the American headquarters and asked for the location of the Polish guard companies, but they weren't helpful at all.

'Let's try Stuttgart,' I said.

We went to Stuttgart via Ulm where the spire of Ulm Cathedral could be seen on the horizon. I was told that the Allies took special care not to bomb the Cathedral. Before we got to Stuttgart, an extra locomotive was attached to help the train up the steep incline.

We didn't stay in Stuttgart; we were travel weary, so took the train to Nurnberg which was like home now. Nights were mainly spent in the waiting room at the railway station, which now and again was raided by American military police. They ordered women at random into their jeeps and were taken to hospital and tested for VD. If positive they were kept in, otherwise they were released.

They took Marga once, but she tested negative, and they brought her back after an hour. I befriended many other girls as I had nothing to do now. I spent most of my time in *Gasthauses* or on the station during the day; at night, either the station or an empty warehouse.

Marga caught me with another girl and set a trap for me. She gave me some cigarettes, then told a military policeman that I was buying on the black-market, which was against the law. I was arrested and sentenced to twenty-eight days in jail. Marga tried to visit me, but I refused to see her.

She came to see me again and again, and eventually she told the prison officer that it was something very important she had to tell me, so I went to see her. She brought me cigarettes, cakes and a very nice shaving kit. Would I forgive her? She only wanted to stop me seeing other women. She knew I was safe and out of harm's way in there. I was glad to see someone anyway. It's not nice in jail.

There was a Latvian in jail for the same offence and a Polish boy, Bronek. The Latvian taught me a song – '*Rotnik rotnik nesper moi spajku ne no pipul mu sa cigaros.*' (The squad leader won't stop my buddy from smoking a cigarette.)

We were released just before Christmas. The prison officer was very friendly. He said, 'Don't let me see you here again.'

He said it in a nice way.

There were six of us released that day. We had all been in the one cell and none of us had any cigarettes, but one of the men had cigarette papers, so we all turned our pockets out and managed to make one thin cigarette which we passed around and had a drag or two each. That was after a good while, as the prison officer outside the door would not give us a light even though he was smoking a pipe. A different officer gave us a light. One of the men told us that a prisoner found a pistol stuffed in the mattress in his cell and tried to smuggle it out of the jail, got caught and was sentenced to five years in prison. That was the norm at that time for possession of a firearm.

The day I was released, Marga was waiting for me outside, gave me some cigarettes and took me for a meal to a *Gasthaus*. We would ride the tram to the edge of town to a smaller railway station waiting room. They were warmer and quieter than the main one, but after a while we had to abandon it as the stationmaster started asking questions. It was a really hard life, wandering from place to place. I often thought, 'If only I had one good meal a day and a nice bed to sleep in, I would work hard all day for it.'

90

Under Suspicion of Murder

We found a nice *Gasthaus* not very far from the Haupt-Bahnhof (railway station) called Beker Her Berge. There was music every night and the waitresses were serving whatever was available that day. We went there often. One night, three plain clothes *Kriminal Polizei* (*Kripo*), came in to check identity documents.

When one of them checked mine, he said, 'Aha! We got him at last.'

They were looking for Stanislaw Wozniak (my false name) who was a truck driver and was wanted for murder. It was about 9pm when they took Marga and me to police headquarters and, under dim lights, a very polite man in plain clothes was asking questions and looking at my documents and photographs until three the next morning. Obviously, it wasn't me they were looking for but my namesake, who was probably out of the country by now. Although I was not guilty, various thoughts went through my mind, knowing that they could pin that one on me like the Russians used to do. It wasn't a pleasant experience. He let us go, and it was back to the waiting room at the station.

The Americans were disbanding more and more guard companies and replacing them with German civilian guards. The Poles, Latvians, Lithuanians and Estonians, who wanted to remain, were placed in DP camps and could immigrate to various countries as displaced persons. At the time, Belgium, France and Australia needed men for the coal mines. I thought Australia was too far, because I thought we would be fighting the Russians pretty soon, so I wanted to be part of that fighting force. I heard that France wasn't very good, so I chose Belgium.

We were issued a displaced person referral card document and put into a transit camp ready to go. Just before we were due to set off, they took the DP slips from us. Unintentionally, while the man was collecting the cards in our room, I was in the toilet, so he missed mine. I thought that it might come in useful later.

91

Belgium, Here I Come

After a long journey on a train, we arrived at a hostel, Frameries Hainaut Rue Jacob, near Mons. The proprietor of the hostel was a Pole who came to Belgium before the war. Our pit (coal mine) was Grantre, about half a mile from the hostel. We started on the afternoon shift. I wasn't impressed. On the morning shift before ours, two men were killed by a rock fall, a Belgian foreman and an Italian miner.

Working in the pit were Poles, Italians, Algerians, Belgians and many German prisoners of war. The management and the foreman were all Belgians. The first day started with the 2pm shift. We were allocated lockers and issued with leather helmets and heavy lamps which hung on the belt. It bruised my leg just above the knee, banging against me as I walked. There were three levels in that pit: 305m, 850m and 950m. I worked at the 950m level.

The lift operator was a huge German prisoner of war. When the lift stopped, we boarded a train, which took us 3km to the coalface. There were so many corridors that I twice lost my way. We were briefed before we went down that no matches, lighters or cigarettes were allowed and, if found, the penalty was one year in jail. We were searched on the way down and when we came back up. Some of the ceilings in the pit were so low that I had to crawl on my stomach or on my knees. The wooden props creaked under the load of the ceiling, and stones and chunks of rock would often fall from above. It wasn't a very pleasant place to work. The train took us so far, then we had to walk quite a distance to the coalface. There were gates in the corridor about every 50yd.

Ventilation was good in the corridors, sounding like a hurricane, until the gates were closed. However, the worked coalfaces had hardly any ventilation. I was provided with a pick hammer, air pipe and a pick and shovel. Coal dug out was shovelled into steel chutes sliding down onto a wide rubber belt which carried it to an outlet which had a steel shutter. As the little railway wagon drew up under it, a man lifted the shutter, and the coal dropped into the wagon below until they were all full, and then the locomotive took it to the lift and up to the surface.

The dust was so thick that the miner's lamp working 10ft away was barely visible. I put a handkerchief around my nose and mouth, but it was hard to breathe. If the air pipe fractured, we had to mend it ourselves, usually tying it up with the handkerchief. After reaching the surface after each shift, we had to hang our tag on a board, put the dirty clothes and the lamp in the locker, shower and then head off to the canteen for a meal which was ready.

Our quarters were rounded, galvanized sheds with bunk beds, one table with benches each side. Full board cost 200 Belgian Francs per week. Anything extra, like beer or cigarettes, we could have on tick and pay at the end of the week. Accommodation money was deducted from our pay. The food was good considering that they had to cater for many different nationalities, all with different tastes. The surroundings were bleak. All I could see on the horizon were slag heaps and coal dust covered the buildings. After the morning shift, I would walk about a mile and a half to sit on a patch of green grass; everything else around was black.

After a couple of weeks, some of us ventured to neighbouring Paturages, where we had a few drinks in a café, a bit like our pubs. Upstairs, there were cubicles where for 50 Francs one could have sex with one of the waitresses. I didn't take advantage of that service and, although there was a language barrier, I found a girl after three weeks.

There was a Russian-speaking fellow who gave the impression that he had plenty of money, and seemed to appear wherever we went. I became suspicious of him because the NKVD had long arms and I thought he might be one of their agents. In one café, there was a portrait of Stalin hanging on the wall. One of our boys, after a few drinks, tried to take it down. A fight developed and they smashed the place.

One weekend we went to Charleroi to see a carnival, and after returning to work found one of the coalfaces completely filled in. Had there been weekend working, twenty miners would have been buried. It was one of the richest seams. The summer of 1947 was very hot, so after a shift, I usually bought two flagons of weak 3 per cent beer, had some food, then usually played cards.

One Sunday, two of the men went on a picnic and didn't return. They told some of the boys that they were going to Spain. They owed the proprietor 12,000 Francs. Quite a few of the men had done the same. I did not like working in the pit. I thought that I will be long enough under the ground when I am dead, so why should I work there now? I was writing to my mother and Marga. I missed Marga a lot. I even wrote a poem to her in German. I sent a letter to Marga saying that I am coming back.

Again, I had a very bad attack of tonsillitis, and I was very ill.

After five days the proprietor's son came and said, 'If you don't go to work tomorrow, there will be no food.'

I was still very ill and had a high temperature. I went to work but didn't work very hard that day and gradually recovered.

92

On the Way Back to Nuremberg

One Sunday, I put a few packets of cigarettes, chocolates and my shaving kit in a bag and went 'on a picnic'. I left my blankets, sleeping bag and other clothes in my room. I caught the train to Liege, which was the nearest station to the German border and the town of Aachen. I had a map and compass and started walking through fields and country tracks in the direction of Aachen. I was chased by a cow in one field and had to run for my life and dived over a hedge. Only just made it. I walked all night. At dawn, I could see the town and walked towards it. Approaching from behind some trees, I walked straight into a border guard several yards in front of me, who was pleasuring himself!

He saw me, and I saw him. I walked straight towards him, and I knew he was embarrassed, which was to my advantage. I told him I was going to see my girlfriend and asked him the shortest route to the station. When he had finished explaining which way I should go, I gave him a packet of cigarettes and proceeded to the station. When I arrived, I was at the end of a long line of people queuing for tickets.

As I reached the ticket booth window, the man behind the counter asked me, '*Haben sie zulasung Karte von die Poliizei?*' (Have you permission from the Police to travel?)

There was still a long queue, so I went back to the end of the line again. This time I got a ticket no questions asked.

When I arrived in Nurnberg, it was like arriving home. I knew the place quite well and there were still some Polish boys 'floating around'. Some intended to stay in Germany; others were waiting to emigrate, and although I had no permanent abode, I did manage to sleep here and there. I bumped into one of the boys from the hospital whose girlfriend, a nurse, Marysia worked there. I asked where he was staying?

'In the bunker', he said.

She said, 'You can come tonight but you will have to sleep with a young Dutch girl medical student who was going to Prague.'

We made love, then she burst into tears. When I woke up, she was gone but had told Marysia that if she got pregnant, she would get rid of it.

Time was no problem, only what to do with it. We would share any money, cigarettes and food with the German boys, who would occasionally steal clothes from washing lines which the German women laundered for American soldiers and officers. They would sell them to buy food and cigarettes.

An amazing thing happened to Marga and I as we were walking past the ruins of a church. Both of us heard sweet, lovely singing coming from that church, but there was nothing there except ruins. We stood there amazed for a while, not comprehending how that could happen. I wonder if anybody else had heard it?

The church was a few hundred yards from the Stork Club. There were dozens of homeless people floating about and casual sex was the norm, sometimes with two or three different women a day. It was a sordid life, moving from *gasthaus* to *gasthaus*, from station to station. Then one time I met Ignacy again and discovered that he was going to the USA, but too late for me as they weren't taking any more for the time being. He said that countries available were France, Venezuela and Britain.

I had heard that France wasn't good, Venezuela was too hot, and so I chose Britain, as one of my distant cousins, Mietek Mularz, was in Edinburgh. I knew this from a letter I had received from my mother. The main emigration office was in Regensburg, so I took the train there and was accepted for Britain. I told some of the boys that I was emigrating to Britain, and they must have told Marga. She came after me begging me to take her with me.

Unfortunately, I could not, even if I had wanted to (which I didn't). She became very ill; it must have been flu. I managed to persuade the officer in charge at the station that she had nowhere to go, and he allowed her to stay. As I was going the next day, she had to go. I took her to the station, and I did feel very sorry for her as she gave me a lot of good times, and besides, she still looked ill. That was the last time I saw my Marga. She left me with many mostly pleasant memories. I did love her.

93

We Are on Our Way to Britain

The next morning, we boarded the lorries and were on our way to a transit camp in Mannheim. When we arrived there, an American commander wouldn't allow us entry into the camp, and after a break, we drove a long way to another transit camp in Munster.

As before, the camp was a disused army barracks with bunk beds, and the food was not good. The transit camp was a mixture of nationalities: Poles, Ukrainians, Latvians, Lithuanians and Estonians. All of us went through rigorous medical checks, five in all. We had to stand naked in a long queue and were checked one by one. When it was my turn, the doctor had a look at me and said, 'You must have had gonorrhoea.' I am still puzzled how he knew just by looking at me.

Anyway, I passed.

One of the men in our room was very strange. He talked in his sleep, acting as if he was possessed by evil spirits. He would draw half human, half animal and devilish faces on the walls and ceiling.

I was really concerned one morning, as I was called to the commandant's office where two men were waiting for me. They asked me my name, which I gave them, '*Stanislaw Wozniak*'. They then asked a few questions and let me go. They must have had a good description of the real Stanislaw Wozniak otherwise they would have questioned me longer. They were *Kripo* or *Kriminal Polizei*.

Many of the Estonians, Ukrainians, Latvians and Lithuanians had either been in the German army, Gestapo and police, or guards in concentration camps and now they were all 'innocent' displaced persons.*

---

* Over 250,000 Ukrainians, 115,000 Latvians and 20,000 Lithuanians served in the German military and security forces in the Second World War.

Their luck was in this far, except for their consciences (if they had any). After all the checks and preparation, we departed on 1 February 1948, and arrived that evening at a British Army post in the Hook of Holland. The soldiers offered us tea with milk in enamel mugs, and that was the first time I had tasted English tea and didn't like it. I was puzzled as to why the British were so crazy about their cup of tea.

We stayed in the army post all night, sat on the floor.

In the morning, we boarded a large ship and headed for England. I felt quite safe now. The NKVD, *Milicja* and the UB were far enough away as not to be a threat. It was the first time I had seen the sea and thought how beautiful it was. It was a very rough journey with big waves lifting the ship up and down and from side to side. Although it was cold, I stayed on deck most of the time. There were quite a few Jewish passengers making their way to Canada. A lot of the men were seasick and vomiting over the side. It was dark when we docked at Harwich (Essex).

94

On English Soil at Last

As we went through the checkpoint, we were given a £1 note, with which I bought a packet of Craven A cigarettes. We were handed some sandwiches and boarded the train for London. We seemed to be travelling for hours through built-up areas. After arriving, we walked a short distance to some hotel, where we were given some food. I can't remember what it was, and this time, we had a bed to sleep on. After smoking some of the Craven A cigarettes, I had a wicked headache as I was used to American cigarettes.

The next morning, we boarded a train which took us to a rest and transit camp at Child's Ercall, near Market Drayton in Shropshire. It was an ex-American army camp. My documents stated that I was destined to be employed at a coalmine in Scotland, but the resettlement officer told me that I didn't have to go there if I didn't want to.

They issued each of us with a ration book with some of the tokens removed. What was left were tokens for chocolate and clothing. Now that all the nationalities were all well mixed up together there was no animosity, except for a remark by one of the Ukrainians that 'We have to beat up the Poles.'

To me, it was all very exciting being in another country and especially England, about which I had heard so much during the war and on whom we had pinned so much hope that they would defeat the Germans.

One of the Latvians was a mandolin player who had played on Riga Radio before the war.

We had one month's rest before departing to our work destinations. Our breakfast was porridge, bread and butter or margarine and coffee. Lunch was mainly cod and mashed potato.

There was always a queue for the bathroom and toilets. One of the Ukrainians only just managed to get out of the bath in time, as the water was extremely hot and he must have had a slight heart attack. He was as red as a lobster.

Many Russians posing as Ukrainians came to Britain.

Our pocket money was five shillings a week (25p) to buy what was available using our ration books, or we could go to what was the equivalent of a disco for 2d (two old pence, or the nearest comparison today is 1p, 1 new pence), which was very cheap. There was nowhere else to go in that area, so I decided to walk to Wellington, which must have been five miles away. I started at 2pm, walking fast through the snow, and got there by 4pm. Had a look around the shops and walked back by 6pm. Just made it for tea. I didn't do it again. I was worn out and was not used to the exertion.

During the day, we passed the time by playing a card game called *Ferbli*, a four-card game similar to poker. Another game we played was pontoon. Win or lose, I enjoyed playing a game of cards. I had been in so many tight spots where my life was at stake, that money did not matter much to me. Easy come, easy go.

I developed a terrible cough and thought I had TB. I didn't bother to see a doctor and I didn't even know if there was one at the camp. Anyway, I wasn't worried all that much about it as the time was approaching for us to go to our places of work. The month was nearly up.

95

Destination Somerset

News came that we were going to Somerset to work on the farms. After a few hours travelling, we arrived at a hostel in a small town on a hill, Wiveliscombe. In the hostel were Polish ex-servicemen and Estonians. They weren't very pleased to see us as they had to make room for us. We had disturbed their routine.

I remember it was Budget time, and cigarettes were increased from 1 shilling and 3 pence (1/3d or 6p today), for twenty large cigarettes like Churchman's No.1, Gold Flake, Embassy, Players, Capstan etc. to 2 shillings and 3 pence (2/3d or 11p today). Our wages were £2, 19 shillings per week, (£2.95p). A tot of gin or whisky was 1 shilling, (5p) so I had a good drink every weekend. We got paid on a Saturday morning. The ex-servicemen were much wealthier than us, as they were given de-mob money. After a week or two they got used to us and treated us as equals.

Every morning, we were taken to work on a committee farm, where we worked with the Land Army girls, which was fun. Some of the men were dropped off at private farms. One evening, I went for a walk and met a nice girl named Joyce and it was my first love of an English girl. It was lovely. After weeks of abstinence from – and inquisitiveness about – English girls, I finally learned.

One Sunday, a Polish priest *(Kapelan)* arrived and held a service in the hall. Being deeply religious, I was moved by the experience as the last time I was at a mass was in a forest in Poland. I was so moved that I couldn't hold back the tears as we sang Polish hymns. It was an extremely emotional occasion for me.

96

On the Move Again

After a few weeks at Wiveliscombe, some of us were moved to a hostel in Crowcombe. This time we were with the Yugoslavs. The change of environment must have had an effect on my cough as it had gone completely. The hostel was a few hundred yards from Crowcombe railway station and the nearest pub was the Stags Head, which was located on the main Taunton to Minehead road and run by two elderly ladies. It was one and a half miles from the hostel. The manager of the hostel was a Mr Lis, a demobbed Polish Army officer of Jewish extraction.

Some of the names I remember were: Jozef Niedziela (ex-*Dragun* or dragoon, a mounted infantry soldier), Frank Garus the lorry driver, Bawel (Paul) Klukowski, Henryk Neuman, who went back to Germany as he could not learn to speak English, Homeniuk Mercer Zielinski, who did not spend one penny in the time I was there. Florko, an ex-forced labour worker in Germany. There were a couple of others whose names I can't remember. Our other lorry driver was an Englishman, an ex-Spitfire pilot.

One of our men, also called Stan, had a slight nervous breakdown and Lis, instead of calling a doctor, called the asylum in Flax Bourton. When his pal went to visit him, Stan told him that he had been beaten with whips. Terrible!

There was a sporting competition between the hostels. The Spitfire pilot was driving the lorry and, on the way back, one of the men leaned against the canvas wall of the lorry and suddenly we heard a crack, and he fell off his seat. The road was narrow and as the lorry swerved, his head hit a telegraph pole and fractured his skull. It was all hushed up and they sent him back to Germany.

Florko always had plenty of money on him, so one Saturday, I borrowed 30 shillings (£1.50) and bought myself quite a nice suit, my favourite colour green. Now with something smart to wear, one evening a few of us went to Taunton for a few drinks and to see a film at the local cinema. While the lorry was waiting to take us back, a large black dog jumped into the lorry and would not go away, so we took it back to the hostel with us. It was a very intelligent animal. I don't know whether it was the tone of the accent, but it could understand Polish. Frank Garus taught it to wake us up in the morning and it went from bed to bed until all of us were up.

Some of us thought we would visit the Stags Head to try the local drinks. Niedziela and I were paired to play darts against a couple of the locals. The price of the game was a pint of draught cider, they called it Razor Blades. We won eight games, and I was dying after eight pints. I couldn't stand the smell of cider for at least two years after that session.

Working near Stogursey one day, I suddenly felt a terrible pain in my chest. Frank had a couple of heavy pushbikes in the lorry. They couldn't leave the job, so he suggested that I take a bike and I rode a little and pushed it a little all the way to Stogumber to see our doctor. When I arrived, there was one woman in the waiting room. He saw her and although I was next, he did not call me in. The waiting room filled up and he made me wait until the last patient had left. He did not examine me or give me anything. Florko was taken to him with severe stomach pains, and he told him to 'jump up and down.'

Obviously, he did not care about foreign patients, only the English. There were other men who needed treatment and did not get any. He was hated by all the hostel residents. I recovered from the illness, no thanks to him, as I was young and active. I used to ride the pushbike around the countryside in my spare time, visiting Williton and Watchet, where I had the best cup of coffee I had ever tasted in an Italian café. Cost 4d, (about 3p).

I used to spend most of my money on cigarettes, whisky and a game of poker at the weekends. Before Henryk Neuman went back to Germany, we would play bridge in the manager's residence. We got on quite well with the Yugoslavs. One of the younger ones, they called the *Kapitan* (Captain), was studying to become a doctor and wherever we went to work he studied his medical notes. I am sure he made it as a doctor. Another of the Yugoslavs was learning to play the accordion but after many complaints, he would practice in the woods nearby.

97

Change of Job

It was in the dining room during teatime that Lis came in and said, 'I need two volunteers for a cook's course'. I thought autumn is coming, and it's no fun on the farm during wet, cold weather. So, I raised my hand, and another fellow volunteered with me. After a few days, we were taken to Wellington in Somerset, where we were taught by an American cook.

After six weeks of intensive instruction, we had exams which included cooking several different meals. I came second out of eight of us. I was then moved to the EVW hostel in Yatton, Somerset, where there were fifty-two men to cook for. One cook, Robert Maska was already there. We were cooking for Poles and Ukrainians who worked on the local farms. The manager of the hostel was John Burton, who lived in one of the buildings with his pretty wife and son, Robert.

Four of us, Robert Maska, Joe Romanczuk, a Ukrainian teacher from Czechoslovakia, Kaluzny, the kitchen porter, and myself, shared a nice room at the end of the building opposite the kitchen. In the office was Mr Wodzinski, an ex-Polish army soldier, a very nice man whose wife had just given birth to a baby daughter. Shortly after, they moved to Glasgow where his wife's father had some property.

Every alternate day, I had to get up at 4am to cut sandwiches, and prepare breakfast for the men, which consisted of sausages, bacon, fried or boiled eggs, porridge and coffee. The next day, I had to cook dinner, tea and supper. After a few days, I asked the chaps if there were any loose women about as I was getting desperate for a bit of sex. They mentioned Ma's Pub in Congresbury, just the other side of the main road, where there will be a girl, Gwen Stocking (nicknamed *Ponczocha*, Polish for stocking) so called because her stockings were always twisted, and she will be at the off licence in a cubicle. They said I should be alright. Sure enough, she was there and on the way to her home through some fields, she gave me a hand job. The next time, and the times after, it was always sex. Apparently, she wouldn't refuse anyone. If I didn't go, she had someone else.

One evening, the boys and I were chatting in the Burtons' living room, talking about ghosts and other strange phenomena, when I said, 'How about the Indian Fuckers', (I meant to say Fakirs) 'who throw a rope in the air, climb it and disappear?' There was a burst of laughter from Mrs Burton, and Robert quietly corrected me.

At the hostel, everything seemed to go smoothly until Mrs Burton went back to her mother. Her and her husband must have been quarrelling. Robert Burton gave me her home address, which was written on a small piece of paper on the table. One evening he came into our room drunk and saw the paper with the address written on it. He went mad, asking me, 'What do you want her address for?'

I said, 'Perhaps I want to send her a birthday card.'

After the row about his wife's address, the atmosphere changed. He went from being friendly to almost hostile. As the working environment was worsening, I thought, it can't be right that I am working eight hours a day, every day, without a day off.

I wrote to the Ministry of Labour, who passed my letter on to the Ministry of Agriculture and Fisheries. Shortly after, I received a large envelope marked 'Private and Confidential', explaining all the rules and regulations about my entitlement. This made the manager even angrier, and he said, 'Even I, as the manager, haven't got the rule book, and they sent you one.'

An ex-serviceman paid us a visit one day and told us that the Walton Park Hotel in Clevedon had job vacancies but the snag was that all aliens had to have permission from the Ministry of Labour to change their employment.

I went to the hostel manager and said, 'Arrange with the labour exchange for me to be able to take the job in the Walton Park Hotel, and I will relinquish my claim for the money which is due to me for the days I should have had off.'

He agreed and made me sign an agreement to that effect. I was glad to sign it and get out of there as the atmosphere was icy. After a week, I received the permission to leave my present job and to go where I wanted. Before I started my new job, I went to Taunton to see some of the men from Crowcombe but, unfortunately, they were all out working so it was a waste of time.

I returned to Clevedon.

My New Job at the Walton Park Hotel

I moved into one of the basement rooms, sharing with an ex-serviceman named Eliasz Paszko, a very pleasant chap who was working as a kitchen porter along with another ex-serviceman, Jan Romanski, a very big fat man. I got on very well with Eliasz. He was a gentleman and was awarded the *Virtuti Militari Cross*, Poland's highest military award for acts of exceptional bravery and military skill whilst fighting in the Battle of Monte Casino.

He came from Gorlice, which isn't far from Glowicnka where I was from. We talked about our war experiences and many other subjects. The hotel manageress was a very smart lady, Mrs Stoken, who instructed me as to what my duties were and what pay I was to receive. My job was in the stillroom, getting the various sized pots of tea and coffee, and jugs of milk and hot water ready. Then there was the toast to make under the very large grill. When the waitresses asked for tea for two, three or four, I had to be quick and watch the toast at the same time. I soon got used to it. Mr Stoken was a fat German of Jewish extraction and Mrs Stoken a French Jew, always smartly dressed and a very efficient organizer. She would change her dresses several times a day, especially if there were a lot of guests. She had an excellent chef, one Frank Harrison, who she looked after well. His wages were £20 a week in 1949 (my wages were £2/15 shillings, £2.75p). She also sent his son, Gary on a chef's course to Paris.

There was quite a turnover of waitress and chambermaid staff. The head porter was a Scotsman, Rob. She started another young man in the stillroom, Victor Chomutov, who said he was Ukrainian, but I guessed he was Russian. I thought he was Yul Brynner, as he had similar features and voice.* His mother and two sisters were going to emigrate to the USA. Three of us shared a room in the basement: Victor, Bob and myself. Victor and I were learning Esperanto and playing the guitar in our spare time. Bob didn't like it when we spoke Polish or Russian, or when we shared a joke he couldn't understand.

My working hours were from 8am to 1.30pm and 6pm to 11pm. The weather was beautiful so every afternoon I was sunbathing and swimming in Lady Bay, which was only 200yd away. The hotel accommodation was good. Clean beds and the food was excellent. One flight of stairs and I was in work.

It was a beautiful summer in 1949, so every Wednesday, my day off, swimming and sunbathing in Lady Bay was the usual routine. One afternoon, the sea was flat as a mirror and I swam out about 50yd. When I turned around to swim back, without realizing it, I was 400yd downstream. When I tried to swim back, I could only stay in the same place as the tide was so strong. I panicked, but after a little thought, I decided to swim with the tide, but cut in towards the beach as the tide was flowing like a river down a narrow channel towards the Clevedon Pier. After a struggle, I managed to reach the beach near the hotel. Sometime later, I witnessed three men and a boy getting into difficulties in the same place. The chef told me that Clevedon had one of the highest tides in the world.

I had a lovely view from the stillroom window, when time allowed, and could watch the ships heading towards Bristol. There was a paddle steamer service from Bristol and Clevedon calling at Weston-super-Mare, Ilfracombe and Cardiff. They were the *Bristol Queen* and *Cardiff Queen*.

---

* Yul Brynner was the famous Russian-American actor and director who starred in productions including *The King and I*.

99

The Beginning of Romance

One Wednesday on my day off, I went for a stroll to town. On the way, I met Beryl Hawkins, who used to visit the hostel occasionally as her father was a friend of the hostel manager, John Burton. Her father was the proprietor of a fish and chip shop in Yatton. Accompanying Beryl was a young lady with dark eyes and very dark hair, a bit older than Beryl. She introduced herself as Nesta Payne from Cardiff. She was on a week's holiday, staying with Reg Hawkins's family.

During the war, Reg stayed with the Payne family when serving in the air force and that's how they knew each other. On one day of Nesta's holiday, her mother Alberta came with her, and we were introduced as we went for a stroll on Clevedon Pier. Shortly, Nesta's holiday ended and she had to go back to Cardiff. I thought that would be the end of our relationship. However, we started corresponding regularly and as Nesta also had Wednesdays off, she would visit me every week.

Sometimes, the paddle steamer only docked at Weston-super-Mare, so I would take the bus to meet her there. Once, I missed the last bus and the last train and had to walk to Clevedon, a long way. The hotel was closed when I got there, so I climbed onto the window ledge and through the window, which was ajar, into my room. The management had a meeting as whether to sack me or not for my unorthodox entry, but my good workmanship must have saved the day.

There were many waitresses and chambermaids working at the hotel but none of them appealed to me. However, I met a beautiful Irish girl from the next hotel who gave me a lovely time. Her name was Cathleen. She warned me that I would be like a wounded soldier after she finished with me, and I was for about three days. She could compete with Marilyn Monroe with her shape and beauty.

There was an attractive Catholic church in Clevedon, which reminded me of the churches in Poland that had a solemn atmosphere. I did not attend mass on Sundays as I was always working.

Bob, the porter, gave me a ticket with some names on and £3 and sent me to an address in a side street. He told me, 'Give it to the man and tell him it's from Bob.' I couldn't get over it, all that money betting on horses when my weekly wage was £2/15 shillings, (£2.75p).

One day a waitress, Mary, proposed to me. She said, 'I will marry you.'

It wasn't going to happen as she wasn't my type. I had good food, a nice room, easy work, good company and a great appetite. What else did I need? At one breakfast, I ate a bowl of porridge, twenty-five sausages (they were delicious), toast and coffee. I was enjoying the chef's oxtail soup one mealtime when I bit through a wasp, which had got into the soup. I didn't get stung but it crunched as I bit into it. It did make me feel sick.

I was moved to another room with the head porter, Bob Scotchman, and Victor Chomutow (who said he was Ukrainian, but I guessed he was Russian as he spoke Russian). He was a nice chap and very determined. He went to a music shop in Bristol with £4 and the guitar he wanted was £6. He would not leave the shop until the shopkeeper let him have it at the lower price. We practised playing in our spare time as well as still learning Esperanto.

I received letters from my mother with news that 'so and so went on tour for so many years', some of them to the 'Rising Sun' (Siberia) and that Blysk was executed. Niemsta (Kazimierz Czlowiekowski) had returned from Siberia due to ill health, but was on the run again. My uncle Antoni Patla was arrested and beaten up. Anyone connected with the Resistance was in danger. The UB were still often visiting my mother asking about me. The Russian motto was, 'Better to arrest a thousand innocents than let one guilty person escape justice.' Many Resistance fighters were arrested, never to return. I had to be extremely careful not to break the law in case I was sent back. I was offended a couple of times but dared not fight.

Over the next year, my romance with Nesta blossomed and we saw each other more frequently. Eventually, I moved in with her parents, Alberta and Ernie, in Cardiff and we were married in June 1951 at St Clare's Catholic Church, Ely, Cardiff.

Epilogue

A note from Len Czekaj, Stanislaw's son

This is where Stan's typed book ends. He continued to write his memoirs in duplicate books and ended up with six volumes, taking his life story up to a couple of weeks before he died.

He wrote them in English, but his handwriting was very difficult to understand, as he wrote them in a sort of English/Polish hand. The paper was very thin, and the writing could be seen through the pages, making it even more difficult to read.

I decided to ask Czeslaw Nowak of the Podkarpakie Museum if they would like all his books, cassette tapes, photographs, medals, and other documents pertaining to his time in the Resistance, and the various organizations in Germany, as they would be better preserved there than in my loft. They arrived during the Covid lockdown, circa 2020–21. His intention was to set up a display for the public showing what people in that area went through. Thank you, Czeslaw.

Over the following pages, I will continue with my father Stan's story from my own memory. The story may not be in chronological order, as I married my wife, Helen in 1975 and we moved from Clarke Street to our own house in Cathays, Cardiff. I was off the scene for a number of years but visited my parents regularly.

Len Czekaj

Life in Cardiff

After marrying Nesta in June 1951, the couple went to live with Nesta's parents, Alberta and Ernest Payne (they called them Bertha and Ernie), at Clarke Street in Ely, Cardiff. Ernie was a train driver, and had worked for British Rail all his life, cycling to and from the Canton Sheds, one of the main British Rail depots. His shift pattern was varied. Stan remembered Ernie working long shifts, starting and ending at all hours of the day and night. Ernie loved his job.

The house in Ely was a bit cramped, as there were two rooms downstairs and three bedrooms upstairs. Stan's first son, Antoni (Toni, named after his uncle), was born on 30 October 1951. I was born in 1952 and named after Nesta's brother, Leonard, as we shared the same birthday, 17 November. When we reached school age, we started at Millbank Primary School, which was just across the street.

Stan was working at Ely Brickworks, a job found for him by Nesta's brother, Leonard (Len Payne). It was hard, dusty and dirty work, and reminded him of the time in the Belgian coal mines. Looking around, he managed to find a job with John Bland & Co Timber Merchant in Splott, working in the hardwood section as a tallyman, estimating costs of various quantities and types of timber which were sold by the cubic foot. He would cycle to work, which was seven miles away, and had to work Saturday mornings, a 42-hour week. The wages were a bit better than the brickworks, although the work was physical, having to load and unload the timber from the lorries.

He was offered one of the company's houses to rent, as the last occupant had passed away. Stan jumped at the chance, as it meant a lot more room, a huge garden and no more cycling the seven miles to work. Conveniently, John Bland's timber yard backed onto the garden of this house. He constructed two ladders, one for each side of the wall, allowing him to climb over the wall and get to work on time. A luxury for him.

Toni and I attended St Albans School, a mile away, and Mum found a job working at C&A, a fashion shop on the main shopping street in the centre of Cardiff. They had more money now, as, before, come Thursday (the day before pay day), they would have just enough for a loaf of bread and ten cigarettes.

Our family lived in Splott for four years, and Stan was able to bring his mother, Anna, over from Poland for a year. Unfortunately, she just couldn't settle down in Wales and decided to return to Poland.

Ernie became ill after slipping and falling on the foot plate of an engine. He carried on regardless and eventually collapsed. He was rushed to hospital and diagnosed with a severe hernia. It had got so bad that they called the family into the hospital, as they knew that he wasn't going to make it. He passed away. This was in 1962.

Bertha was now on her own, and she asked my parents if they would go back to Clarke Street to live. We did, and we now had the larger room downstairs and the two larger bedrooms, one for Toni and myself, and the other for Nesta and Stan. He joined the British Legion club and made friends with another Polish family, George and Phyllis Wisnieski. Over the coming years, we spent many a Christmas, Sunday evenings and holidays with them.

It was now 1964 and Mum was pregnant again. She was in hospital for several weeks, diagnosed with thrombosis in one of her legs. Bertha was looking after us and Stan had to continue working. Things were getting a bit strained between Bertha and Stan, and we were missing Mum. Andrew was born in January 1965. Eventually, after a few more weeks, Mum came home with baby Andrew.

The sleeping arrangements were starting to get difficult, as Andrew had to share the bedroom with my parents, which was fine when he was a baby, but as the years went by, Stan found himself sleeping downstairs on a camp bed. (This arrangement lasted until I married

Helen in 1975, and then Andrew moved in with Toni.) At that time, 1965, I was attending St Francis School at the top of Ely, whilst Toni went to Lady Mary School in Cyncoed, Cardiff. I started at St Illtyd's Grammar School, Cardiff, in September that year, having to travel from one end of Cardiff to the other.

John Bland Closing

Stan had some bad news. John Bland's was closing. He needed another job. His guardian angel was on his side again. Paddy Dee, whom he had many dealings with over the years, was now working for a timber merchants in Cardiff, Magnet Southern Ltd, and he said, 'We need someone in the hardwood section.' Stan took the job.

In 1968, Toni left school and went to work in the John Williams foundry (which closed in 1990). He worked there for a couple of years and decided that it wasn't for him. With no job, Stan suggested that Toni come and work for Magnet Southern in the timber cutting section, which he did.

Magnet Southern was a shambles. He remembers that the washing facilities for the workers in the yard was a dirty old towel hanging over a dirty sink, and no soap. It didn't change until he threatened to get the health and safety executive involved. Timber would go missing left, right, and centre. There was no system in place to check what came in and what went out. Just guess work. Some of the lads were fleecing the company in the region of hundreds of pounds in missing timber.

In 1969, I left school and got a position as a trainee chemical technician at BP Chemicals at Barry, but after two years was made redundant. In 1971, I managed to get a trainee technician post at the University of Wales Institute of Science and Technology.

Transport for Work

Stan decided that he needed some transport to get to work, as he was getting older and cycling back and forth just did not appeal to him anymore. Enter the Raleigh Runabout moped – basically, a bicycle with a 50cc engine, and totally inadequate bicycle front brakes. He rode this to work for a couple of years, and would go fishing some evenings from Penarth beach, about seven miles from home.

One night he had a puncture and decided to take a short cut through some fields and a wood. Big mistake. Trying to haul the moped through trees and shrubs nearly killed him. He had to retrace his steps back to the main road and push the moped home. Nesta was going spare. He got home well after midnight. The moped kept getting punctures and he decided to park it in the shed and forget it.

The Yamaha 50cc

My father Stan then decided to go for something a little more up to date, and found a Yamaha 50cc for sale on a postcard placed in the window of the post office. He contacted the fellow selling the bike and struck a deal. I was wary of the chap and knew him to be a bit untrustworthy. It turned out that he still owed some money to the loan company, and was hoping to sell the bike without telling them. Anyway, it was sorted out and Stan had the bike. He tested it by riding around the garden until he got used to it. Bang! It blew a head gasket and the engine was shot. Back to the Raleigh Runabout.

Stan decided that he must progress and started taking driving lessons. He passed his test on the second attempt. He needed a car.

Cortina Mark 1

Bertha had a friend in Worthing with whom she would stay for a few weeks each year. Her husband had passed away and the car, a Ford Cortina Mark 1 that he alone drove, was parked on the drive of their bungalow. A letter arrived for Bertha, asking if Stan wanted to buy the car. All he had to do was drive it from Worthing to Cardiff. Tax and insurance were in place. Simple, or so he thought. A few days before he was due to travel to Worthing, he trapped a nerve in his back and couldn't even stand up. He had to lie on the floor, as this was the only position which gave him any relief from the pain.

Bertha contacted the son of a friend of hers, Dudley Pearce. He and I took the train to Worthing and, after an hour trying to start the car, Dudley drove it back to Cardiff with Bertha's friend in the back seat and myself in the front.

It was a few days before he could inspect his new purchase. The car wasn't very reliable and had persistent niggling faults. After a couple of years, he sold the Cortina to some lads who wanted a restoration project and bought Alf Sims's Vauxhall estate. A much better vehicle. Alf was our coalman for many years. Some months went by and the lads who bought the Cortina brought it back to show him what they had done to it. It was in pristine condition and fully restored.

Stan owned several used cars over the next few years, including a Rover 2000, an Austin Maxi and an Austin Princess. He always wanted a Mercedes, but that one eluded him. The Rover was the worst one by far, needing lots of repair work.

Enjoy It Today

Growing up, Stan was working a 44-hour week, which meant we didn't see him a great deal and he would visit the Royal British Legion some evenings, much to Nesta's disgust. He did have an attitude of 'enjoy it today, as you don't know what tomorrow will bring.'

He was terrible handling money, and that was always a bone of contention between my father and mother. He would give Mum her housekeeping for the week and burn his payslip so no one could see what he earned. Payday was a Friday and, by Wednesday or Thursday, he would be asking Nesta for some of the housekeeping money, saying 'I will pay you back on Friday'. I do remember a couple of instances where they nearly split up because of arguments over money. He could also be a jealous person, sometimes accusing Mum of fancying other men, which she never ever did.

Trip to Poland

Stan had been writing to his mother since he had arrived in Britain, being extremely careful what he wrote in his letters. His mother also wrote in a coded way, as all letters were opened and censored.

Stan kept every letter from his mother, and there were bundles of them tied up and kept in the sideboard. Unfortunately, they were burned sometime after Stan had passed away as nobody could read Polish. They would have provided an insight as to what life was like in Poland in the years after the war.

Now it was time to chance a trip back home. Flights, hotels and visas were sorted. Stan, Nesta and Andrew set off for two weeks' holiday. Andrew must have been about 12 years old, which would have been 1977. Toni and I were both married, and no longer living at home.

At this point, Poland was still under the communist regime. They were surprised at the poverty the people of Poland were enduring, compared to the lifestyle they had back home. There were shortages of most basic items, and a sense of complete control by the authorities. I remember Stan telling me that he was a bit concerned when travelling around that he might be arrested for his previous misdemeanours, so he didn't tell any of his relatives that he was coming to visit. They turned up on his mother's doorstep unannounced. You can imagine what a complete surprise it must have been for Anna.

They met up with as many of Stan's friends and relations as they could, who were still around. They all survived the trip.

Back in Cardiff, we used to have a Polish priest visit now and again, and Stan would be acquiescent in his presence. Very unlike Stan. It stemmed from his strict Catholic upbringing – the priests in Poland were treated like gods. What us boys found amusing was that the Polish priest would only visit to scrounge 'offerings for the church'. We boys and Mum would make ourselves scarce when he was in the house, hiding in another room or upstairs. Stan would then come in and ask Mum for some money to give the priest to bless the house, as he never had a penny left over. Bit of a con.

Occasionally, Stan would visit the Polish House in Newport Road, Cardiff, to meet with other Poles. He was friends with a Polish watchmaker who had a shop in Cardiff, I think his surname was Uruski. I was in the same school as his son. I remember the time when Pope John Paul, who was Polish, visited Cardiff on 2 June 1982. Stan was really excited. The Pope celebrated mass in Pontcanna Fields and Stan was there.

Andrew Is Becoming a Problem

Andrew, being the youngest and the only one of the brothers living at Clarke Street, was treated like an only child having far more freedom than Toni and I ever had. He was spoilt, having everything he wanted.

He pestered my parents to allow him to attend the local comprehensive school, which was Glyn Derw High School in Ely, Cardiff, as his dodgy friends went there. He and his friends were always in trouble when they actually attended school. They were caught shooting the glass insulators from electricity pylons when they should have been in school. The police were involved. Of course, they were full of regret once they had been caught.

Stan was badly affected by Andrew's behaviour, especially when he would go missing for hours and come home stinking of glue. Stan could tell which glue he had used by the smell. Glue sniffing to get high was common at that time. The glue was poured into a crisp packet and the fumes sucked in. Stan would go looking for Andrew in the local woods at the dead of night and drag him home.

I remember Stan telling me that he woke up one night and thought that someone's arm was trying to grab him. He beat the arm on the bedside cabinet, only to realize that it was his own, which had become numb due to him lying on it. He could barely move his arm for weeks afterwards. He started developing a nervous twitch. This was the effect Andrew was having on him. Nesta wanted to throw Andrew out of the house as he was so disruptive. Stan would have none of it. This was a bone of contention, and I could sense the distance between them with every visit.

Sadly, Andrew's troubles continued into his teens and later years, culminating in him dying in 2012, aged 47, through drink and drugs.

Made Redundant Again

Magnet Southern sold out and Stan was made redundant again in the mid-1980s. He was in his early sixties. He now retired. He liked to work but found himself with very little to do. He made some benches for the garden and basically pottered around.

Some Bad News

A letter arrived from Poland. Anna Czekaj was found dead floating in a river. Stan was devastated as the letter was a few weeks old and his mother's funeral had taken place. There was nothing he could do. He thought that she might have been driven to drown herself due to having to live with one of the relatives, but there was no chance of proving anything.

Some Worse News

My father had been complaining for some time about a mole on his foot that was growing and would not heal no matter what ointments he put on it. After much nagging by Nesta, he saw his doctor who referred him to a skin specialist. I took him to see the dermatologist and I asked him what he had said. 'I will tell you when we get back to the house', he said.

He was diagnosed with malignant melanoma, which had spread from his foot up to his thigh. It's the only time I have seen my father cry. The specialist told him he may have two years if he was lucky. Initially, the surgeons removed part of his foot hoping to stem the spread. This was too little too late.

Helen and I contacted his MP, Rhodri Morgan, and asked if there was any treatment available. He must have contacted some specialist, who offered to give Stan a 'perfusion' procedure, which entailed disconnecting the affected leg and pumping chemotherapy chemicals through the tissue to kill the cancerous growths, then reattaching the leg.

The date was set and Stan reluctantly agreed. Two days before the procedure, Stan found that the cancer had spread to his other leg. The operation was cancelled, and he was told that there was nothing they could do.

It's a terrible disease. Swellings the size of golf balls were spreading all over his body. They would bleed and he would spend an hour just dressing them.

The final years of Stan's life were really dominated by his illness. Stan's demeanour changed when he found out that he was on borrowed time. He could be quite contentious and liked a good argument. He was not always considerate towards Nesta until the bad news, which was like throwing a switch. He became more caring and amenable towards her and more relaxed.

A Visitor from Poland

At about that time, Stan had a letter from Poland asking if one of his distant relations could visit him. Her name was Halina and she was in her late 20s. Stan had to stand guarantor for her and she stayed with Nesta, Stan and Andrew at their house in Cardiff. Stan was over the moon initially, and when she arrived, he was in tears.

She was a strange girl as she would just stay in her room and not mix with the family. She got a job cleaning and kept every penny to herself, whilst Stan and Nesta supported her with meals and lodgings for free. Stan would – at a great effort, as he was on crutches due to his illness – drive her to her place of work and pick her up every day. He was really suffering at that time, as he was breaking out in large lumps all over his body which seeped and bled.

As time went on, they had to tell her that she had to leave as she became a big drain on the household resources and, eventually, she went back to Poland.

A Trip to Lourdes, the Last Hope

St Clare's Catholic Church in Ely had arranged a trip to Lourdes in France for the sick. Stan wanted to go. With two walking sticks and a wheelchair, he boarded the coach and visited the place in Lourdes where the Virgin Mary is said to have appeared, and those who saw her were cured of fatal illnesses.

He wasn't well cared for on that trip, and Mum told me that none of his dressings had been changed the whole time he was away. The trip didn't have the desired effect and probably weakened him.

Now the cancer was more painful, spreading even further. I remember seeing his fingers so swollen that they were the size of bread rolls. It spread to his head, and he started acting totally out of character. He would spend most of his time in bed.

Holme Towers

The doctor made an appointment for Stan to have an assessment at Holme Towers in Penarth, a hospice for people who have terminal illness. I drove him and Mum there, and they explained the procedure for patients and visitors. About a week later, I got a call at work. It was Mum.

'You had better get to our house quick as your father is much worse,' she said.

We called the doctor and he asked me, 'It's your decision. Do you want Stan to go to Holme Towers?'

It was the hardest decision I have ever had to make, as Holme Towers is the end of the line. It was 1 August 1990.

We visited Stan as often as we could. His birthday was Friday, 10 August, and we took him some flowers and a balloon with '66' written on it, as he wasn't eating or drinking much. I said to him, 'We will see you again on Sunday as George Wisnieski is calling in to see you tomorrow.'

Sunday, 12 August at 6am, the phone rang. The voice on the other end said, 'Stan has passed away.'

The requiem mass was a couple of weeks later with Father Ritco, a Polish priest conducting the service in Polish to a packed church. Father Jones conducted some of the service in English. At the graveside, a contingent of Polish Partisans sang some Polish songs as the coffin was lowered into the ground. Stan is buried at Western Cemetery, Ely, Cardiff.

Final Reflections

In Stan's final years, big changes were happening across Europe. In 1989, shortly before he died, the Berlin Wall was torn down, communism lost its grip over Eastern Europe, and Poland regained its independence. Although he was aware, these changes arrived too late for Stan to really appreciate, as at that time he was fading fast.

For his actions in the war, Stan was awarded the Home Army Cross (*Krzyż Armii Krajowej*) as a member of the Polish Home Army, and the Cross of Valour (*Krzyż Walecznych*) given to those who have 'demonstrated deeds of valour and courage on the field of battle'.

Stan received acknowledgement of the medals in 1970 and 1985. They would have been awarded by the Polish Government-in-Exile in London, as in that timeframe, the Resistance still wasn't recognized by the communist government of the People's Republic of Poland. This was rectified in 1992, when the newly-independent democratic Polish government passed an act finally giving these honours official recognition.

My father never really told us much about his time in the Resistance until Toni, Andrew and myself were older. As highlighted earlier in the book, during his time living under occupation in the Polish Resistance, Stan regularly existed in a kill-or-be-killed environment, not knowing if he would survive from day to day. His outlook on life was shaped by these brutal experiences.

I remember him telling me how he had to shoot the two Russians that stopped him, and describing the gore created by the bullets as they penetrated the Russian's skull, as told earlier in the book. He also mentioned having to shoot the Gestapo collaborator, and the fact that he was starving most of the time. The episode with his hands getting burnt also came up on Bonfire Nights, warning us of the risks of fireworks.

All in all, Stan was contented with his lot, as it was hugely better than his time during the war. He loved his boys. He had a home, family, work and he took great pleasure having the odd bet on horseracing and bingo.

He hated guns and knives.

Alojzy Czekaj (1892–1925)

Stan's father, Alojzy Czekaj, was wounded and taken prisoner during the First World War. His capture was notified on 18 May 1916. He was incarcerated in the Russian prisoner-of-war camp at Nikolaevsk (modern Pugachev) in the Samara Oblast (district) of the Volga region of Russia.

He was taken prisoner near Dubno, in western Ukraine, during the fighting that led up to a major Russian offensive in June 1916, as described in the Austro-Hungarian casualty lists published during the First World War, and held in the Austrian National Library in Vienna. The Russians made no real preparation for dealing with prisoners of war and treated them poorly, with no effective system of provision of food and medical care. Alojzy was one of the lucky ones as he survived Russian captivity. However, systematic incompetence and neglect by the Russian authorities resulted in over 350,000 Austro-Hungarian soldiers dying in Russian captivity between 1914 and 1918.

Alojzy is recorded as 'Alois Czekaj' in the military archive, which is not such a surprise as Alois is the German rendering of Alojzy. Before the collapse of the Austro-Hungarian Empire, it was common practice for Slavonic names to be recorded in their Germanic form on official documents.

Records show that he was *Gefreiter* or Lance Corporal in No 3 Company, 1st Battalion, *Kaiserlich-Königliche* (Imperial Royal) *Landwehr* (Territorial Force) (Przemyśl) Infantry Regiment No 18 (K.K.LIR 18). As he was born in 1892, he was probably called up for military service in 1912 for three years with the colours. However, as war broke out before his discharge, his service was extended for the duration of hostilities.

His regiment's headquarters was in the strategically important fortress town of Przemyśl in Austrian Galicia, as that area of what is now southeastern Poland was then called. Like all *Landwehr* regiments in the Austrian portion of the Austro-Hungarian Empire, his regiment had three 1,000-man battalions and was ethnically 47 per cent Ruthenian (Ukranian), 43 per cent Polish, and 10 per cent other.

I suspect that the 1st Battalion (Alojzy's battalion) was primarily made up of Polish soldiers and, although the official language of command would have been Austrian German – hence the German form of his first name – its working language would have been Polish. The regiment was part of 89th *Landwehr* Infantry Brigade, 45th *Landwehr* Infantry Division, X Corps which was part of the Austro-Hungarian 1st Army.

Alojzy's unit took part in the bloody battles for Galicia in 1914, as well as the fighting around Przemyśl in 1915. It was probably captured in late April or early May 1916, in fighting around Sandomierz and Tarlo Jozefow, in a part of eastern Poland that was then part of Russian Poland at the time.

My Brother, Toni

After writing this memoir, I have decided to write about my brother, Toni, who passed away on 24 November 2025, aged 74 (I guess I am now an only child, aged 73.) I did not know that Toni was ill and was told the day before he died. Helen, his wife, arranged the funeral for 16 December 2025. All the children were there: David, Christopher and Michael, with Christopher's son, Ellistan (or E.J.) and Michael's two children, Kingsley and Nyah. Several old friends known as the 'Benny Boys' attended; so-called because back in the early 1970s seven of them including Toni spent a boozy fortnight in Benidorm.

It is such a shame that Toni will never read Stan's memoir. Rest in peace, Toni, my Brother. You will never be forgotten.